KIDS ASK THE DARNDEST THINGS

ABOUT GOD AND THE HISTORY

KIDS ASK THE DARNDEST THINGS ABOUT GOD AND THE HISTORY
COPYRIGHT © 2009 BY BALL PUBLICATIONS. ALL RIGHTS RESERVED.

COVER DESIGN BY WANDA BALL. COPYRIGHT © 2009 ALL RIGHTS RESERVED.

NO PART OF THIS BOOK MAY BE REPRODUCED OR TRANSMITTED IN ANY FORM BY ANY MEANS, GRAPHIC, ELECTRONIC, OR MECHANICAL, WITHOUT WRITTEN PERMISSION IN WRITING FROM THE PUBLISHER, EXCEPT BY A REVIEWER WHO MAY QUOTE BRIEF PASSAGES IN A REVIEW.

SCRIPTURE TAKEN FROM THE HOLY BIBLE, NEW INTERNATIONAL VERSION®. COPYRIGHT © 1973, 1978, 1984 BY INTERNATIONAL BIBLE SOCIETY. USED BY PERMISSION OF INTERNATIONAL BIBLE SOCIETY.

"NIV" AND "NEW INTERNATIONAL VERSION" ARE TRADEMARKS REGISTERED IN THE UNITED STATES PATENT AND TRADEMARK OFFICE BY INTERNATIONAL BIBLE SOCIETY.

PUBLISHED 2009. PRINTED BY CAFEPRESS.COM IN THE UNITED STATES OF AMERICA

ISBN
978-0-9800069-1-9

KIDS ASK THE DARNDEST THINGS ABOUT GOD AND THE HISTORY

ANSWERS FROM THE NEXT TWELVE BIBLE BOOKS OF HISTORY

WANDA L. BALL

BALL PUBLICATIONS CHRISTIAN BOOKS™
CHINO, CALIFORNIA

ACKNOWLEDGMENTS

I would like to thank to my husband, for his continued support. To my son, who is still my inspiration for my second book. To my mother, who has contributed to this book with her motivational minutes. To my dad for continuing to be the rock. To Pastor James Ellis and Claudette, of New Beginnings Baptist Church, Riverside, CA. for allowing me to use my ministry to glorify God. And to my family and friends, who give me encouraging words along the way.

THANK YOU!

Contents

ACKNOWLEDGMENTS

JOSHUA - GOD THE SAVIOR

1) WHY DID JOSHUA SEND TWO MEN TO SPY ON JERICHO?.....2
2) WHY DID REHAB, THE INNKEEPER, HIDE THE SPIES.....4
3) HOW DID GOD STOP THE JORDAN RIVER FROM FLOWING?.....6
4) WHY DID THE TWELVE PRIESTS HAVE TO GATHER TWELVE STONES FROM THE RIVER?.....8
5) HOW COME THE ISRAELITES HAD TO MARCH AROUND THE CITY OF JERICHO FOR SEVEN DAYS?.....10
6) HOW CAN THE SUN STAND STILL AND THE MOON STOP?.....12
7) HOW DID GOD ALLOW JOSHUA TO CONQUER THE REMAINING LAND AT AN OLD AGE?.....14
8) WHY DID JOSHUA GIVE A FAREWELL SPEECH TO THE ISRAEL LEADERS?.....16
9) HOW CAN A STONE BE A WITNESS?.....18
10) WHY DID THEY BURY JOSHUA IN THE PROMISED LAND?.....20

JUDGES - RULERS

11) WHY WAS JUDAH THE PERSON CHOSEN TO FIGHT THE CANAANITES?.....24
12) WHY DID THE ISRAELITES NEED JUDGES?.....26
13) WHO WAS THE PROPHETESS, DEBORAH? AND WHY DID SHE SING A SONG?.....28
14) HOW DID GIDEON DEFEAT THE MIDIANITES?.....30
15) HOW COULD ABIMELECH KILL SIXTY NINE OF HIS BROTHERS WITH ONE STONE?.....32
16) WHY WAS SAMSON A MIRACLE CHILD?.....34
17) HOW CAN SAMSON KILL A THOUSAND MEN WITH A JAWBONE OF A DONKEY?.....36
18) WHY DID SAMSON LOSE HIS GREAT STRENGTH AND THEN GET IT AGAIN?.....38
19) WHY DID THE ISRAELITES FIGHT THE BENJAMITES?.....40
20) HOW DID THE REMAINING BENJAMITES "CATCH" A NEW WIFE?...42

RUTH - A STORY OF LOYALTY

21) WHY DID NAOMI WANT HER TWO DAUGHTER-IN-LAWS TO GO BACK TO THEIR HOMES?.....46
22) HOW DID RUTH MEET BOAZ?.....48
23) WHY DID RUTH LIE DOWN AT BOAZ'S FEET?.....50
24) HOW CAN TAKING OFF YOUR SANDAL AND GIVING IT TO ANOTHER, MAKE A DEAL FINAL?.....52
25) HOW CAN NAOMI, THE WIDOWER, HAVE A SON?.....54

1 SAMUEL - ASKED OF GOD

26) HOW WAS SAMUEL'S BIRTH SPECIAL?.....58
27) WHY DID GOD PUT A CURSE ON THE HOUSE OF ELI, THE PRIEST?.....60
28) WHY DID THE PEOPLE OF ISRAEL ASK FOR A KING?.....62
29) WHY DIDN'T SAUL WANT TO BE KING?.....64
30) HOW COULD THE LORD REJECT SAUL AS KING?.....66
31) WHY DID DAVID'S HARP MAKE SAUL FEEL BETTER?.....68
32) HOW CAN A BOY KILL A GIANT WITH ONE STONE?.....70
33) WHY DID DAVID LIVE IN PHILISTINE ENEMY TERRITORY?.....72
34) WHY DID SAUL ASK A WITCH FOR HELP?.....74
35) HOW COULD SAUL TAKE HIS OWN LIFE?.....76

11 SAMUEL - ASKED OF GOD 2

36) WHY WAS DAVID ANOINTED KING OVER JUDAH?.....80
37) HOW DID DAVID BECOME KING OVER ISRAEL?.....82
38) WHY DID GOD MAKE A PROMISE TO DAVID?.....84
39) WHY DID THE PROPHET NATHAN CURSE DAVID?.....86
40) WHY DID DAVID'S SON, ABSALOM, KILL HIS BROTHER, AMNON?...88
41) HOW COME ABSALOM CONSPIRED AGAINST HIS FATHER DAVID?...90
42) WHY DID ABSALOM FIGHT AGAINST HIS FATHER, KING DAVID?.....92
43) WHY DID DAVID LIVE IN PHILISTINE ENEMY TERRITORY?.....94
44) HOW COME GOD GAVE DAVID THREE CHOICES OF PLAGUES ON ISRAEL?.....96
45) WHY DID DAVID HAVE TO BUILD GOD AN ALTAR?.....98

1 KING - THE KINGDOM UNITED

46) WHY DID DAVID'S SON, ADONIJAH, TRY TO BE THE NEW KING?.....102
47) WHY DID KING SOLOMON KILL HIS BROTHER ADONIJAH?.....104
48) HOW COME GOD GAVE KING SOLOMON GREAT WISDOM?.....106
49) WHY WAS SOLOMON GOING TO CUT A BABY IN HALF?.....108
50) WHY DID IT TAKE SOLOMON THIRTEEN YEARS TO BUILD HIS PALACE?.....110
51) HOW CAN SOLOMON HAVE SEVEN HUNDRED WIVES?....112
52) HOW DID ONE OF SOLOMON'S OFFICIALS BECOME KING?.....114
53) HOW CAN A MAN BE FED BY RAVENS?.....116
54) HOW DID ELIJAH BRING THE WIDOW'S SON BACK TO LIFE?.....118
55) HOW DID KING AHAB DIE FROM A STRAY BOW AND ARROW?.....120

11 KING - THE KINGDOM DIVIDED

56) HOW DID ELIJAH GO TO HEAVEN IN A TORNADOE?.....124
57) HOW DID THE SHUNAMMITE BOY COME BACK FROM THE DEAD?....126
58) HOW CAN A HUNDRED PEOPLE EAT WITH TWENTY LOAVES OF BREAD?.....128
59) WHY DID HAZAEL MURDER HIS MASTER, KING BEN-HADAD?.....130
60) HOW CAN JOASH BECOME KING AT SEVEN YEARS OLD?.....132
61) WHY DID GOD TAKE THE ISRAELITES FROM THEIR HOMELAND?....134
62) HOW CAN THE ANGEL OF THE LORD KILL A HUNDRED AND EIGHTY-FIVE THOUSAND ASSYRIAN MEN?.....136
63) WHY DID GOD GIVE KING HEZEKIAH FIFTEEN MORE YEARS TO LIVE?.....138
64) HOW WAS THE BOOK OF THE LAW FOUND?.....140
65) WHY DID GOD ALLOW JERUSALEM TO BE CAPTURED?.....142

1 CHRONICLES - WORDS OF THE DAYS

66) WHAT IS A GATE KEEPER?.....146
67) WHY DID KING SAUL HAVE TO DIE?.....148
68) WHY DID GOD HAVE THE LEVITES BRING UP THE ARK OF THE LORD TO JERUSALEM?.....150
69) HOW COME DAVID WANTED HIS SON SOLOMON TO BUILD A TEMPLE FOR THE LORD?.....152
70) WHY DID DAVID PRAY IN FRONT OF EVERYONE?.....154

11 CHRONICLES - WORDS OF THE DAYS CONTINUED

71) HOW CAN GOD TURN INTO A DARK CLOUD?.....158
72) WHY DID GOD APPEAR TO SOLOMON?.....160
73) WHY DID THE QUEEN OF SHEBA GIVE KING SOLOMON GIFTS?.....162
74) WHY DID ASA, THE KING OF JUDAH, REFORM HIMSELF?.....164
75) HOW DID KING JEHOSHAPHAT DEFEAT THE MOABITES AND AMMONITES?.....166

EZRA - BORN IN CONFUSION

76) WHY DID CYRUS, THE KING OF PERSIA, HELP THE PEOPLE RETURN TO JERUSALEM?.....170
77) WHY DID PEOPLE OPPOSE THE REBUILDING OF THE TEMPLE?.....172
78) HOW DID THE TEMPLE FINALLY GET COMPLETED?.....174
79) WHY DID KING ARTAXERXES OF BABYLON, LET EZRA TAKE ALL THE ISRAELITES BACK TO JERUSALEM?.....176
80) WHY WAS EZRA ANGRY ABOUT SOME OF THE ISRAELITE MARRIAGES?.....178

NEHEMIAH - COMFORTER OF GOD

81) WHY DID NEHEMIAH WANT TO REBUILD THE WALL OF JERUSALEM?.....182
82) WHY DID SANBALLAT AND TOBIAH OPPOSE REBUILDING THE WALL?.....184
83) WHY DID THE ISRAELITES CRY WHEN EZRA READ THE BOOK OF THE LAW?.....186
84) HOW COME THE ISRAELITES MADE A NEW AGREEMENT WITH GOD?.....188
85) WHY DID NEHEMIAH HAVE TO REFORM THE ISRAELITES AGAIN?.....190

ESTHER - THE HIDDEN STAR

86) WHY DID KING XERXES TAKE AWAY QUEEN VASHTI'S CROWN?.....194
87) HOW DID ESTHER, A JEW, BECOME QUEEN?.....196
88) WHY DID HAMAN WANT TO KILL ALL OF THE JEWISH PEOPLE?....198
89) WHY DID KING XERXES KILL HAMAN?.....200
90) WHY DID THE JEWS CELEBRATE PURIM?.....202

JOSHUA - GOD THE SAVIOR

WHY DID JOSHUA SEND TWO MEN TO SPY ON JERICHO?

ANSWER:

This was part of the land that God promised to the Israelites. He wanted Joshua to send two spies to check out the land, in order to make sure it was safe for them to enter. And also to determine how they would defeat the king and his people.

Scripture Reference: Joshua 2:1

"Then Joshua son of Nun secretly sent two spies from Shittim. "Go, look over the land, he said, "especially Jericho." So they went and entered the house of a prostitute named Rahab and stayed there."

MOTIVATIONAL MINUTE: When trouble rushes in and interrupts your plans, be obedient to God - ask Him to help you be calm, cool, and steady.

WHY DID REHAB, THE INNKEEPER, HIDE THE SPIES?

Answer:

When the king of Jericho heard that the spies were staying at the inn, he sent a message for Rehab to release them to him. She didn't want to release them, so she told the messenger that they were no longer there. She did this, because she had heard about the miracles and defeats of other cities that God had performed. She wanted her family to be saved after the Israelites defeated Jericho.

Scripture Reference: Joshua 2:4

"But the woman had taken the two men and hidden them. She said, "Yes, the men came to me, but I did not know where they had come from."

Motivational Minute: Confess your need to God, and ask Him to deliver you.

HOW DID GOD STOP THE JORDAN RIVER FROM FLOWING?

Answer:

When the Israelites set out to defeat Jericho, God told Joshua that He would perform a miracle to show the Israel people that He would be with him, like He was with Moses. Joshua told twelve priests, who carried the covenant of the Lord, to go and stand in the Jordan River. And as soon as they stepped foot in the river, its' waters stopped and stood up in a heap. This allowed the Israelites to cross the river on dry land, just like they had crossed the Red Sea in Egypt. And as soon as all were across, God allowed the water to flow freely again.

Scripture Reference: Joshua 3:13, 17

"The priests who carried the ark of the covenant of the Lord stood firm on dry ground in the middle of the Jordan, while all Israel passed by until the whole nation had completed the crossing on dry ground."

Motivational Minute: God wants to change things for you. But He is waiting for your total cooperation.

WHY DID THE TWELVE PRIESTS HAVE TO GATHER TWELVE STONES FROM THE RIVER ?

ANSWER:

AFTER THE ISRAELITES CROSSED THE RIVER ON DRY LAND, JOSHUA WANTED THE PRIESTS TO EACH COLLECT A STONE FROM THE MIDDLE OF THE JORDAN TO BE A MEMORIAL TO THE PEOPLE AND TO THEIR DESCENDANTS FOREVER. AND GOD ALSO WANTED THEM TO KNOW THAT HE WAS POWERFUL AND TRUE TO HIS WORD.

SCRIPTURE REFERENCE: JOSHUA 4:5-6

"AND SAID TO THEM, "GO OVER BEFORE THE ARK OF THE LORD YOUR GOD INTO THE MIDDLE OF THE JORDAN. EACH OF YOU IS TO TAKE UP A STONE ON HIS SHOULDER, ACCORDING TO THE NUMBER OF THE TRIBES OF THE ISRAELITES, TO SERVE AS A SIGN AMONG YOU. IN THE FUTURE, WHEN YOUR CHILDREN ASK YOU, "WHAT DO THESE STONES MEAN?"

MOTIVATIONAL MINUTE: AS A BELIEVER, YOU ARE MEANT TO ENJOY YOUR SPIRITUAL INHERITANCE.

HOW COME THE ISRAELITES HAD TO MARCH AROUND THE CITY OF JERICHO FOR SEVEN DAYS?

Answer:

ONCE JOSHUA AND THE ISRAELITES MADE IT TO THE CITY OF JERICHO, THEY HAD TO DEVELOP A PLAN OF ATTACK. SO THE LORD TOLD JOSHUA TO TELL THE PEOPLE TO WALK AROUND THE WALLS OF THE CITY ONE TIME FOR SIX DAYS. ON THE SEVENTH DAY, THEY HAD TO WALK AROUND SEVEN TIMES. AFTER THE SEVENTH TIME, THE TRUMPETS WOULD SOUND AND JOSHUA WOULD COMMAND THE PEOPLE TO GIVE A LOUD SHOUT IN ORDER FOR THE WALL TO COLLASPE. AFTER THE PEOPLE DID THIS FOR SEVEN DAYS THE WALL COLLASPED AND THE ISRAELITES CHARGED IN AND DEFEATED THE CITY OF JERICHO JUST AS GOD TOLD THEM.

SCRIPTURE REFERENCE: JOSHUA 6:3-5

"MARCH AROUND THE CITY ONCE WITH ALL THE ARMED MEN. DO THIS FOR SIX DAYS. HAVE SEVEN PRIESTS CARRY TRUMPETS OF RAMS' HORNS IN FRONT OF THE ARK. ON THE SEVENTH DAY, MARCH AROUND THE CITY SEVEN TIMES, WITH THE PRIESTS BLOWING THE TRUMPETS. WHEN YOU HEAR THEM SOUND A LONG BLAST ON THE TRUMPETS, HAVE ALL THE PEOPLE GIVE A LOUD SHOUT; THEN THE WALL OF THE CITY WILL COLLAPSE AND THE PEOPLE WILL GO UP, EVERY MAN STRAIGHT IN ."

MOTIVATIONAL MINUTE: SELDOM DO YOUR CIRCUMSTANCES CHANGE WITHOUT SOMETHING FIRST CHANGING IN YOU.

HOW CAN THE SUN STAND STILL AND THE MOON STOP?

ANSWER:

THE PEOPLE FROM THE CITY OF GIBEON HAD HEARD ABOUT THE DESTRUCTION OF THE OTHER CITIES AND WANTED TO BE SPARED. SO THEY PRETENDED TO COME FROM A FAR AWAY LAND SO THEY COULD MAKE A TREATY OF PEACE WITH JOSHUA. JOSHUA BELIEVED THEM AND PROMISED TO PROTECT THEM FROM DEATH AND FROM OTHER CITIES WHO MIGHT ATTACK THEM. WHEN THE GIBEONITES WERE ATTACKED BY THE KINGS OF JERUSALEM, HEBRON, JARMUTH, LACHISH AND EGLON, WITH GOD'S HELP, JOSHUA AND HIS PEOPLE CAME TO THEIR RESCUE. WHILE THEY WERE BEING DEFEATED, JOSHUA SAID TO THE LORD IN THE PRESENCE OF ISRAEL TO LET THE SUN STAND STILL AND THE MOON TO STOP UNTIL THE DEFEAT WAS OVER. AND THERE HAS NEVER BEEN A DAY LIKE IT BEFORE OR AFTER, A DAY WHEN THE LORD LISTENED TO A MAN.

SCRIPTURE REFERENCE: JOSHUA 10:12-14

"ON THE DAY THE LORD GAVE THE AMORITES OVER TO ISRAEL, JOSHUA SAID TO THE LORD IN THE PRESENCE OF ISRAEL: "O SUN, STAND STILL OVER GIBEON, O MOON, OVER THE VALLEY OF AIJALON." SO THE SUN STOOD STILL, AND THE MOON STOPPED, TILL THE NATION AVENGED ITSELF ON ITS ENEMIES, AS IT IS WRITTEN IN THE BOOK OF JASHAR. THE SUN STOPPED IN THE MIDDLE OF THE SKY AND DELAYED GOING DOWN ABOUT A FULL DAY. THERE HAS NEVER BEEN A DAY LIKE IT BEFORE OR SINCE, A DAY WHEN THE LORD LISTENED TO A MAN. SURELY THE LORD WAS FIGHTING FOR ISRAEL!...."

MOTIVATIONAL MINUTE: EXPECT GOD TO BRING GOOD OUT OF EVERY CIRCUMSTANCE IN YOUR LIFE. WHATEVER HAPPENS, TRUST IN THE LORD.... AND TRUST IN THE POWER OF HOPE!

HOW DID GOD ALLOW JOSHUA TO CONQUER THE REMAINING LAND AT AN OLD AGE?

ANSWER:

AFTER JOSHUA HAD DEFEATED A TOTAL OF THIRTY ONE KINGS, GOD TOLD HIM HE STILL HAD VERY LARGE AREAS OF LAND THAT HAD TO BE TAKEN OVER. BECAUSE JOSHUA WAS VERY OLD, AND COULDN'T DEFEAT EVERYONE, GOD DROVE OUT THE PEOPLE OF THE MOUNTAIN REGIONS HIMSELF. AFTER THIS WAS DONE, JOSHUA WAS ABLE TO FINISH DIVIDING THE TERRITORIES OF LAND AS GOD PROMISED THEM BEFORE HE DIED.

SCRIPTURE REFERENCE: JOSHUA 13:1, 6

"WHEN JOSHUA WAS OLD AND WELL ADVANCED IN YEARS, THE LORD SAID TO HIM, "YOU ARE VERY OLD, AND THERE ARE STILL VERY LARGE AREAS OF LAND TO BE TAKEN OVER...."

MOTIVATIONAL MINUTE: CALM DOWN, CHEER UP, AND LEARN TO ENJOY THE INHERITANCE THAT IS YOURS THROUGH CHRIST.

WHY DID JOSUA GIVE A FAREWELL SPEECH TO THE ISRAEL LEADERS?

ANSWER:

Since Joshua knew he would die soon, he decided to gather all of the leaders of the tribes together to discuss all of God's promises that were fulfilled. He wanted them to continue to obey the laws of Moses and to not associate with other nations that didn't believe. If they violated the laws, then God wouldn't be with them and protect them.

SCRIPTURE REFERENCE: JOSHUA 23:1-5

"After a long time had passed and the Lord had given Israel rest from all their enemies around them, Joshua, by then old and well advanced in years, summoned all Israel - their elders, leaders, judges and officials- and said to them: "I am old and well advanced in years"... you yourselves have seen everything the Lord your God has done to all these nations for your sake; it was the Lord your God who fought for you...."

MOTIVATIONAL MINUTE: God wants you to enjoy everyday life - it is His will for you.

HOW CAN A STONE BE A WITNESS?

ANSWER:

After Joshua assembled all of the leaders together, he went over all that God had done, from the time of Moses to the present. After he was done, he asked them if they would continue to serve God. The people assured Joshua that they would do so. So he took a large stone and set it up under a tree near God's holy place. And the stone became a "witness" against them if they were ever untrue to their word.

SCRIPTURE REFERENCE: JOSHUA 24:26-27

"And Joshua recorded these things in the book of the law of God. Then he took a large stone and set it up there under the oak near the holy place of the Lord. See! he said to all the people. This stone will be a witness against us. It has heard all the words the Lord has said to us. It will be a witness against you if you are untrue to your God."

MOTIVATIONAL MINUTE: Don't let the devil steal the thrill of your righteousness through Christ.

WHY DID THEY BURY JOSHUA IN THE PROMISED LAND?

Answer:

After Joshua died at the age of a hundred and ten years old, they buried him in the land he inherited. He was buried at Shechem in the tract that Jacob bought. This became the inheritance of Joseph's descendants, which was the land promised by God.

Scripture Reference: Joshua 24:32

"And Joseph's bones, which the Israelites had brought up from Egypt, were buried at Shechem in the tract of land that Jacob bought for a hundred pieces of siver from the sons of Hamor, the father of Shechem. This became the inheritance of Joseph's descendants."

Motivational Minute: God is eager to reveal today's plan for you.

JUDGES - RULERS

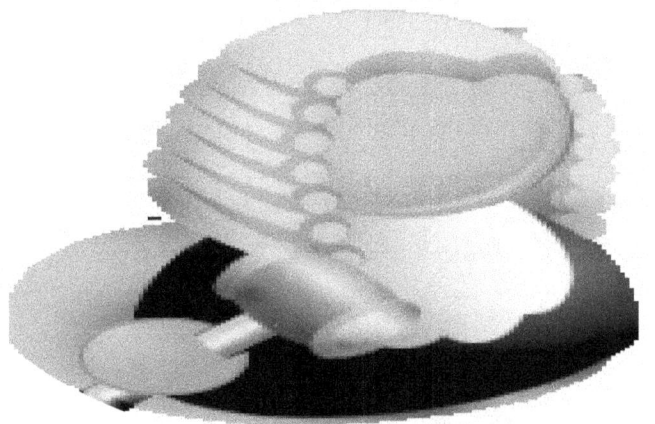

WHY WAS JUDAH CHOSEN TO FIGHT THE CANAANITES?

Answer:

After Joshua died, the people of Israel asked the Lord who would be the person to lead them. The Lord chose Judah to lead them and to fight the remaining Canaanites. Judah's men also asked the Simeonites to help them and once they agreed, they were able to defeat ten thousand men and their king, Adoni-Bezek.

Scripture Reference: Judges 1:1-2

"After the death of Joshua, the Israelites asked the Lord, "Who will be the first to go up and fight for us against the Canaanites?" The Lord answered, "Judah is to go; I have given the land into their hands.""

Motivational Minute: God may not lay out a blueprint for your day, but He will direct your path, if you acknowledge Him in all of your ways.

WHY DID THE ISRAELITES NEED JUDGES?

ANSWER:

Before Joshua died, the people vowed that they wouldn't worship any other idols or Gods. They remembered what God had done for them and all of the tribes that they were able to defeat. But once Joshua died, the people went back to their old ways and worshipped other gods. Because they did this, the Lord became very angry and decided to stop protecting them from their enemies. Because the people were in great distress, God decided to give the people judges, or leaders, to save them from their enemies. But the people still wouldn't listen to them and continued to do evil. After all of the judges died, and the people continued to do evil, God decided not to protect them from their enemies anymore. He wanted to teach the Israelites a lesson who had not fought in any wars in Canaan.

SCRIPTURE REFERENCE: JUDGES 2:16-19

"Then the Lord raised up judges, who saved them out of the hands of these raiders. Yet they would not listen to their judges but prostituted themselves to other gods and worshiped them..." "But when the judge died, the people returned to ways even more corrupt than those of their fathers, following other gods and serving and worshiping them. They refused to give up their evil practices and stubborn ways."

MOTIVATIONAL MINUTE: God conquers evil with good by pouring out His limitless grace upon you. So that if you sin, His grace becomes greater than your sin.

WHO WAS THE PROPHETESS DEBORAH? AND WHY DID SHE SING A SONG?

ANSWER:

AFTER THE PEOPLE OF ISRAEL CONTINUED TO DO EVIL, THEY WERE SOLD TO JABIN, A KING OF CANAAN. BECAUSE THEY WERE OPPRESSED FOR TWENTY YEARS, BY HIS COMMANDER SISERA, THEY ASKED GOD FOR HELP. DEBORAH, A PROPHETESS, LEAD ISRAEL AT THAT TIME. SHE ASKED BARAK FROM KADESH, TO DEFEAT JABIN'S ARMY. HE AGREED, BUT ASKED HER TO GO WITH HIM. AND IN DOING SO, SHE SAID THE LORD WOULD ALLOW A WOMAN TO DEFEAT THEM. AFTER GOD ALLOWED THEM TO DEFEAT KING JABIN AND HIS COMMANDER, SISERA, THEY SANG A SONG PRAISING GOD, TO THE PEOPLE OF ISRAEL. THEN THEY HAD PEACE AGAIN FOR FORTY YEARS.

SCRIPTURE REFERENCE: JUDGES 4:4-5, 5

"DEBORAH, A PROPHETESS, THE WIFE OF LAPPIDOTH, WAS LEADING ISRAEL AT THAT TIME. SHE HELD COURT UNDER THE PALM OF DEBORAH BETWEEN RAMAH AND BETHEL IN THE HILL COUNTRY OF EPHRAIM, AND THE ISRAELITES CAME TO HER TO HAVE THEIR DISPUTES DECIDED."

MOTIVATIONAL MINUTE: IF YOU ARE STRUGGLING WITH EMOTIONAL DISTRESS OR A BROKEN HEART, GOD WANTS TO RENEW YOUR MIND, RESTORE YOUR SOUL, AND GIVE YOU A FRESH START.

HOW DID GIDEON DEFEAT THE MIDIANITES?

ANSWER:

THE ISRAELITES CONTINUED TO DO EVIL AND FOR SEVEN YEARS, THE MIDIANITES WERE ALLOWED TO RULE OVER THEM. THE PEOPLE ONCE AGAIN, ASKED GOD FOR HELP. SO GOD ANNOINTED GIDEON, WHOSE CLAN WAS THE WEAKEST AND WAS THE LEAST IN HIS FAMILY. GOD TOLD GIDEON TO ONLY TAKE THREE HUNDRED MEN TO MIDIAN AND HE WOULD HELP HIM DEFEAT THEM. AFTER THEY SURROUNDED THE CAMP, THE MEN BLEW THEIR TRUMPETS, BROKE THEIR JARS AND SHOUTED "FOR THE LORD AND FOR GIDEON." THE MEN OF MIDIAN TURNED AGAINST EACH OTHER AND KILLED THEMSELVES. AND GIDEON CAPTURED AND DEFEATED LEADERS, OREB AND ZEEB AND THE KING'S OF MIDIAN, ZEBAH AND ZALMUNNA, JUST AS GOD PROMISED. THE LORD PROTECTED THE ISRAELITES AGAIN FOR FORTY YEARS UNTIL GIDEON DIED.

SCRIPTURE REFERENCE: JUDGES 7:7-8, 22

"THE LORD SAID TO GIDEON, "WITH THE THREE HUNDRED MEN THAT LAPPED I WILL SAVE YOU AND GIVE THE MIDIANITES INTO YOUR HANDS. LET ALL THE OTHER MEN GO, EACH TO HIS OWN PLACE..." "WHEN THE THREE HUNDRED TRUMPETS SOUNDED, THE LORD CAUSED THE MEN THROUGHOUT THE CAMP TO TURN ON EACH OTHER WITH THEIR SWORDS. THE ARMY FLED TO BETH SHITTAH TOWARD ZERERAH AS FAR AS THE BORDER OF ABEL MEHOLAH NEAR TABBATH."

MOTIVATIONAL MINUTE: YOU'RE SPECIAL; YOU HAVE WORTH AND VALUE... BELIEVE IT, RECEIVE IT, AND BE ALL YOU CAN BE IN CHRIST.

HOW COULD ABIMELECH KILL SIXTY NINE OF HIS BROTHERS WITH ONE STONE?

ANSWER:

BEFORE GIDEON DIED HE HAD SEVENTY SONS WITH HIS WIVES AND ONE SON NAMED ABIMELECH, WITH HIS SLAVE GIRL. AFTER GIDEON DIED, ABIMELECH WENT TO HIS MOTHER'S BROTHERS AND CONVINCED THEM THAT THEY SHOULD HAVE ONE RULER INSTEAD OF SEVENTY, BECAUSE HE WAS THEIR FLESH AND BLOOD. AFTER THEY AGREED, HE WENT TO HIS FATHER'S HOME AND KILLED SIXTY NINE BROTHERS WITH ONE STONE. BUT HIS YOUNGEST BROTHER, JOTHAM, WAS ABLE TO HIDE. AFTER HE RULED OVER ISRAEL FOR THREE YEARS, GOD SENT AN EVIL SPIRIT TO COME BETWEEN ABIMELECH AND THE CITIZENS OF SHECHEM, BECAUSE OF THE CRIME THEY COMMITTED. AFTER THEY FOUGHT AGAINST EACH OTHER, ABIMELECH EVENTUALLY WAS KILLED AND THE MEN OF SHECHEM CONTINUED TO BE CURSED BY GOD.

SCRIPTURE REFERENCE: JUDGES 9:1-2, 5

"ABIMELECH SON OF JERUB-BAAL (GIDEON) WENT TO HIS MOTHER'S BROTHERS IN SHECHEM AND SAID TO THEM AND TO ALL HIS MOTHER'S CLAN. ASK ALL THE CITIZENS OF SHECHEM, "WHICH IS BETTER FOR YOU: TO HAVE ALL SEVENTY OF JERUB-BAAL'S SONS RULE OVER YOU, OR JUST ONE MAN?" REMEMBER, I AM YOUR FLESH AND BLOOD." ..."HE WENT TO HIS FATHER'S HOME IN OPHRAH AND ON ONE STONE MURDERED HIS SEVENTY BROTHERS, THE SONS OF JERUB-BAAL. BUT JOTHAM, THE YOUNGEST SON OF JERUB-BAAL, ESCAPED BY HIDING."

MOTIVATIONAL MINUTE IF YOU WANT TO BE SENSITIVE TO GOD'S LEADING, LEARN TO FOLLOW PEACE.

WHY WAS SAMSON A MIRACLE CHILD?

ANSWER:

BECAUSE THE ISRAELITES CONTINUED TO DO EVIL, THE PHILISTINES WERE ALLOWED TO RULE OVER THEM FOR FORTY YEARS. GOD DECIDED TO GIVE THEM ANOTHER CHANCE, SO HE SENT HIS ANGEL TO APPEAR TO A MAN ANAMED MANOAH AND HIS WIFE, WHO WERE UNABLE TO HAVE CHILDREN. HE TOLD THEM THAT THEY WOULD HAVE A SON WHO WOULD DELIVER THE ISRAELITES OUT OF SLAVERY FROM THE PHILISTINES. THE ONLY CONDITIONS OF HER PREGNANCY WERE TO NOT DRINK WINE, EAT ANYTHING UNCLEAN AND TO NOT CUT HIS HAIR AFTER HE WAS BORN. BECAUSE SHE DID EVERYTHING THAT WAS ASKED, SHE GAVE BIRTH TO HER MIRACLE CHILD, SAMSON.

SCRIPTURE REFERENCE: JUDGES 13:2-5

"A CERTAIN MAN OF ZORAH, NAMED MANOAH, FROM THE CLAN OF THE DANITES, HAD A WIFE WHO WAS STERILE AND REMAINED CHILDLESS. THE ANGEL OF THE LORD APPEARED TO HER AND SAID, "YOU ARE STERILE AND CHILDLESS, BUT YOU ARE GOING TO CONCEIVE AND HAVE A SON. NOW SEE TO IT THAT YOU DRINK NO WINE OR OTHER FERMENTED DRINK AND THAT YOU DO NOT EAT ANYTHING UNCLEAN, BECAUSE YOU WILL CONCEIVE AND GIVE BIRTH TO A SON. NO RAZOR MAY BE USED ON HIS HEAD, BECAUSE THE BOY IS TO BE A NAZIRITE, SET APART TO GOD FROM BIRTH, AND HE WILL BEGIN THE DELIVERANCE OF ISRAEL FROM THE HANDS OF THE PHILISTINES."

MOTIVATIONAL MINUTE: SET YOUR FAITH AND TRUST IN GOD AND WATCH TO SEE IF HE WILL TURN IT AROUND FOR YOUR GOOD.

HOW CAN SAMSON KILL A THOUSAND MEN WITH A JAWBONE OF A DONKEY?

Answer:

As Samson grew up, he became very strong. And he wanted to marry a Philistine woman. Samson's parents were worried because the Philistines ruled over them. But because it was God's will, they agreed. When Samson went to visit the family of his bride, a lion tried to attack him, but Samson tore the lion apart with his bare hands. After he got to the camp, he told her family a riddle and if they could answer it within seven days, he would reward them with thirty sets of clothing. Because the Philistines couldn't figure out the riddle, they asked his new bride to try to get the answer from him. She tricked him and he gave her the answer. Because of his anger, he killed thirty men and removed their clothes and gave them to the Philistines. As a result, the father of the bride gave her away to a friend. When Samson found out his bride was given away and eventually killed, he set their camp on fire. The Philistines captured Samson and tried to tie him up with rope. Once the Spirit of God came over him, he was able to break through the rope and grab a jawbone of a donkey and kill a thousand men. Samson was able to lead Israel for the next twenty years.

Scripture Reference: Judges 15:14-16

"As he approached Lehi, the Philistines came toward him shouting. The Spirit of the Lord came upon him in power. The ropes on his arms became like charred flax, and the binding dropped from his hands. Finding a fresh jawbone of a donkey, he grabbed it and struck down a thousand men. Then Samson said, "With a donkey's jawbone I have made donkeys of them. With a donkey's jawbone I have killed a thousand men."

Motivational Minute: You have desires of the flesh, but you also have desires inspired by the Holy Spirit.

WHY DID SAMSON LOSE HIS GREAT STRENGTH AND THEN GET IT AGAIN?

Answer:

AFTER SOME TIME, SAMSON FELL IN LOVE WITH A WOMAN FROM GAZA, NAMED DELILAH. AFTER THE PHILISTINE RULERS FOUND OUT SAMSON WAS THERE, THEY TRIED TO CAPTURE HIM. KNOWING THAT HE HAD GREAT STRENGTH, THEY ASKED DELILAH TO FIND OUT THE SECRET TO HIS GREAT STRENGTH AND THEY WOULD PAY HER. SO AFTER A NUMBER OF TRIES, SAMSON FINALLY TOLD HER THAT IF HIS HAIR WAS CUT, HIS STRENGTH WOULD GO AWAY. SO DELILAH TOLD THE PHILISTINES HIS SECRET AND ONCE HE FELL ASLEEP, THEY CUT OFF SEVEN BRAIDS OF HIS HAIR, SUBDUED HIM AND BLINDED HIM IN BOTH EYES. AFTER HE WAS IMPRISONED FOR SOME TIME, HIS HAIR BEGAN TO GROW BACK. WHILE THE PHILISTINES CELEBRATED, THEY WANTED SAMSON TO PERFORM FOR THEM. AS HE WAS PERFORMING, HE ASKED A SERVANT TO HELP HIM TO PUT HIS HANDS ON THE PILLARS THAT SUPPORTED THE TEMPLE. THE TEMPLE HELD APPROXIMATELY THREE THOUSAND MEN, WOMEN AND THEIR RULERS. THEN SAMSON PRAYED TO GOD ONE LAST TIME TO RESTORE HIS STRENGTH IN ORDER TO GET REVENGE FOR BLINDING HIM. GOD ALLOWED HIM TO PUSH DOWN THE TEMPLE AND HE DIED ALONG WITH EVERYONE THERE.

SCRIPTURE REFERENCE: JUDGES 16:4-6, 17, 25-30

"SOME TIME LATER, HE FELL IN LOVE WITH A WOMAN IN THE VALLEY OF SOREK WHOSE NAME WAS DELILAH. THE RULERS OF THE PHILISTINES WENT TO HER AND SAID, "SEE IF YOU CAN LURE HIM INTO SHOWING YOU THE SECRET OF HIS GREAT STRENGTH AND HOW WE CAN OVERPOWER HIM SO WE MAY TIE HIM UP AND SUBDUE HIM. EACH ONE OF US WILL GIVE YOU ELEVEN HUNDRED SHEKELS OF SILVER...." "SO HE TOLD HER EVERYTHING. "NO RAZOR HAS EVER BEEN USED ON MY HEAD," HE SAID, "BECAUSE I HAVE BEEN A NAZIRITE SET APART TO GOD SINCE BIRTH. IF MY HEAD WERE SHAVED, MY STRENGTH WOULD LEAVE ME, AND I WOULD BECOME AS WEAK AS ANY OTHER MAN."

MOTIVATIONAL MINUTE: GOD DOESN'T GET TIRED, AND THE WORD SAYS HE GIVES POWER TO THE FAINT AND WEARY, AND INCREASES STRENGTH TO THOSE WHO HAVE NO MIGHT.

WHY DID THE ISRAELITES FIGHT THE BENJAMITES?

Answer:

A LEVITE MAN FROM EPHRAIM, MARRIED A WOMAN FROM BETHLEHEM. SHE WAS UNFAITHFUL TO HIM AND LEFT HIM AND WENT BACK TO LIVE WITH HER FATHER. AFTER FOUR MONTHS, THE MAN TRIED TO PERSUADE HER TO COME BACK AND AFTER SEVERAL DAYS, SHE AGREED. ONCE THEY LEFT TO GO BACK HOME TO EPHRAIM THEY STOPPED IN GIBEAH TO REST. THEY STAYED IN AN OLD MAN'S HOUSE FOR THE NIGHT. ONCE THERE, A GROUP OF BAD MEN CAME TO THE DOOR TO KILL THE LEVITE. INSTEAD OF HIM GOING OUTSIDE, HE GAVE THEM HIS WIFE AND THEY KILLED HER INSTEAD. AFTER THE LEVITE RETURNED HOME, HE TOLD ALL OF THE OTHER ISRAEL TRIBES WHAT HAPPENED AND THEY DECIDED TO SEEK REVENGE ON THOSE MEN. ONCE THEY ALL RETURNED, THE BENJAMITES WOULDN'T SURRENDER THE BAD MEN AND DECIDED TO GO TO WAR. AFTER THE THIRD TRY, THE LORD GAVE THE ISRAELITE TRIBES THE POWER TO DEFEAT THE BENJAMITES AND THEY WON.

SCRIPTURE REFERENCE: JUDGES 20:4-8

"SO THE LEVITE, THE HUSBAND OF THE MURDERED WOMAN, SAID, "I AND MY CONCUBINE CAME TO GIBEAH IN BENJAMIN TO SPEND THE NIGHT. DURING THE NIGHT THE MEN OF GIBEAH CAME AFTER ME AND SURROUNDED THE HOUSE, INTENDING TO KILL ME. THEY RAPED MY CONCUBINE, AND SHE DIED.... NOW, ALL YOU ISRAELITES, SPEAK UP AND GIVE YOUR VERDICT. ALL THE PEOPLE ROSE AS ONE MAN, SAYING, NONE OF US WILL GO HOME. NO, NOT ONE OF US WILL RETURN TO HIS HOUSE."

MOTIVATIONAL MINUTE: EVERYTHING THAT WE RECEIVE FROM GOD COMES BY FAITH.

HOW DID THE REMAINING BENJAMITES "CATCH" A NEW WIFE?

Answer:

After the war between the Israelites and the Benjamites was over, six hundred Benjamites were able to get away. The Israelites were very upset that the Benjamite tribe betrayed them and they vowed to not give their daughters to them in marriage. But because these men were spared and they wanted to restore peace amongst the tribes, they knew they needed wives to have new families and rebuild their people. They discovered that no one from the Jabesh Gilead tribe had come to worship the Lord, so they decided to kill everyone there except the virgins. After doing so, there were four hundred young women spared, which wasn't enough after they were given to the Benjamites. So they told the remaining men to go to the annual festival of the Lord in Shiloh and "catch", or take a wife, while they danced. And by doing so, no one broke the vow.

Scripture reference: Judges 21:15-16, 20-21, 23

"The people grieved for Benjamin, because the Lord had made a gap in the tribes of Israel. And the elders of the assembly said, "With the women of Benjamin destroyed, how shall we provide wives for the men who are left?"...."So they instructed the Benjamites, saying, "Go and hide in the vineyards and watch. When the girls of Shiloh come out to join in the dancing, then rush from the vineyards and each of you seize a wife from the girls of Shiloh and go to the land of Benjamin."...."So that is what the Benjamites did. While the girls were dancing, each man caught one and carried her off to be his wife...."

Motivational Minute: Accept the free gift of God's grace and allow Him to change your life into the peaceful, abundant life He has planned for you.

RUTH - A STORY OF LOYALTY

WHY DID NAOMI WANT HER TWO DAUGHTER-IN-LAWS TO GO BACK TO THEIR HOMES ?

ANSWER:

NAOMI AND HER HUSBAND, ELIMELECH WENT TO LIVE IN THE COUNTRY OF MOAB, BECAUSE OF A FAMINE IN BETHLEHEM. THEY HAD TWO SONS NAMED, MAHLON AND KILION AND WHILE LIVING THERE, MARRIED MOABITE WOMEN NAMED, ORPAH AND RUTH. NOAMI'S HUSBAND AND TWO SONS DIED, SO ALL OF THEM BECAME WIDOWED. NAOMI DECIDED TO GO BACK TO HER HOME IN BETHLEHEM. AND SHE ENCOURAGED HER DAUGHTER-IN-LAWS TO GO BACK HOME WHERE THEY COULD FIND OTHER HUSBANDS AND REBUILD THEIR LIVES. ORPAH AGREED, BUT RUTH BEGGED NAOMI TO GO WITH HER, UNTIL SHE AGREED.

SCRIPTURE REFERENCE: RUTH 1:8-9, 14

"THEN NAOMI SAID TO HER TWO DAUGHTERS-IN-LAW, "GO BACK, EACH OF YOU, TO YOUR MOTHER'S HOME. MAY THE LORD SHOW KINDNESS TO YOU, AS YOU HAVE SHOWN TO YOUR DEAD AND TO ME. MAY THE LORD GRANT THAT EACH OF YOU WILL FIND REST IN THE HOME OF ANOTHER HUSBAND."..."AT THIS THEY WEPT AGAIN. THEN ORPAH KISSED HER MOTHER-IN-LAW GOOD-BY, BUT RUTH CLUNG TO HER."

MOTIVATIONAL MINUTE: ACCEPT GOD'S LOVE FOR YOU AND MAKE THAT LOVE THE BASIS FOR YOUR LOVE FOR OTHERS.

HOW DID RUTH MEET BOAZ?

ANSWER:

WHILE RUTH WAS LIVING IN BETHLEHEM WITH NAOMI, SHE WORKED IN THE FIELD PICKING UP LEFT OVER GRAIN. THE OWNER OF THE FIELD, WAS A MAN NAMED BOAZ, WHO WAS A RELATIVE OF NAOMI'S HUSBAND. BOAZ WENT TO GREET THE HARVESTERS AND NOTICED RUTH WORKING IN HIS FIELD. WHEN HE ASKED HIS FOREMAN WHO SHE WAS, HE TOLD HIM THAT SHE WAS THE WOMAN WHO CAME BACK FROM MOAB WITH NAOMI. HE WAS SO IMPRESSED WITH HER LEAVING HER HOME AND LIVING AMONG PEOPLE SHE DIDN'T KNOW, THAT HE WANTED TO MEET HER AND REPAY HER. AFTER MEETING WITH HER, HE ALLOWED HER TO EAT UNTIL SHE WAS FULL AND GATHER MORE GRAIN AND BARLEY THAN SHE COULD CARRY BACK TO NAOMI.

SCRIPTURE REFERENCE: RUTH 2:5-6

"BOAZ ASKED THE FOREMAN OF HIS HARVESTERS, "WHOSE YOUNG WOMAN IS THAT?" THE FOREMAN REPLIED, "SHE IS THE MOABITESS WHO CAME BACK FROM MOAB WITH NAOMI."

MOTIVATIONAL MINUTE: IF YOU WAIT UNTIL EVERYTHING IS PERFECT BEFORE REJOICING AND GIVING THANKS, YOU WON'T HAVE MUCH FUN.

WHY DID RUTH LIE DOWN AT BOAZ'S FEET?

Answer:

Since Boaz was related to Naomi's late husband and such a good man, she wanted Ruth to marry him. So she hinted for Ruth to go to the place where he would be winnowing barley on the floor and wait for him. After he finished eating and laid down, she uncovered his feet and laid down also. When he discovered her, he asked why she was there. She told him that she would like to be married. Boaz told her that there was another relative who was entitled to marry her first. If he refused, then he would surely marry her. So she stayed there until morning.

Scripture Reference: Ruth 3:2-5

"Is not Boaz, with whose servant girls you have been, a kinsman of ours? Tonight he will be winnowing barley on the threshing floor. Wash and perfume yourself, and put on your best clothes. Then go down to the threshing floor, but don't let him know you are there until he has finished eating and drinking. When he lies down, note the place where he is lying. Then go and uncover his feet and lie down. He will tell you what to do. "I will do whatever you say," Ruth answered. So she went down to the threshing floor and did everything her mother-in-law told her to do."

Motivational Minute: Many people love things and use people to get them. But God intends for you to love people and use things to bless them.

HOW CAN TAKING OFF YOUR SANDAL AND GIVING IT TO ANOTHER, MAKE A DEAL FINAL?

ANSWER:

ONCE BOAZ REALIZED THAT HE WANTED TO MARRY RUTH AND ACQUIRE HER LAND, HE SPOKE WITH THE RELATIVE WHO WAS ENTITLED TO HER LAND FIRST. ONCE THE RELATIVE REALIZED THAT HE COULDN'T TAKE OVER THE LAND AND MARRY RUTH, HE ALLOWED BOAZ TO DO SO. SO THE RELATIVE TOOK OFF HIS SANDAL AND GAVE IT TO BOAZ AS A METHOD OF LEGALIZING THE TRANSFER OF PROPERTY IN ISRAEL. THEN BOAZ ANNOUNCED TO THE ELDERS AND EVERYONE THERE THAT HE HAD BOUGHT THE LAND FROM NAOMI AND ACQUIRED RUTH AS HIS WIFE.

SCRIPTURE REFERENCE: RUTH 4:5-8

"THEN BOAZ SAID, "ON THE DAY YOU BUY THE LAND FROM NAOMI AND FROM RUTH THE MOABITESS, YOU ACQUIRE THE DEAD MAN'S WIDOW, IN ORDER TO MAINTAIN THE NAME OF THE DEAD WITH IS PROPERTY..." "SO THE KINSMAN-REDEEMER SAID TO BOAZ, "BUY IT YOURSELF." AND HE REMOVED HIS SANDAL."

MOTIVATIONAL MINUTE: A TRUE LOVE WALK DOES NOT COME EASILY OR WITHOUT PERSONAL SACRIFICE, BUT THE BENEFITS ARE GREAT.

HOW CAN NAOMI, THE WIDOWER, HAVE A SON?

ANSWER:

AFTER BOAZ AND RUTH MARRIED, THEY HAD A SON NAMED OBED. RUTH PRAISED GOD, BECAUSE HE ALLOWED HER TO HAVE A SON TO CARRY ON THE FAMILY NAME. HER SON WAS ABLE TO RENEW NAOMI'S LIFE AND SUSTAIN HER IN HER OLD AGE. SHE BECAME SO CLOSE TO OBED, THAT THE WOMEN SAID, "NAOMI HAS A SON."

SCRIPTURE REFERENCE: RUTH 4:13-17

"SO BOAZ TOOK RUTH AND SHE BECAME HIS WIFE. THEN HE WENT TO HER, AND THE LORD ENABLED HER TO CONCEIVE, AND SHE GAVE BIRTH TO A SON. THE WOMEN SAID TO NAOMI: "PRAISE BE TO THE LORD, WHO THIS DAY HAS NOT LEFT YOU WITHOUT A KINSMAN-REDEEMER. MAY HE BECOME FAMOUS THROUGHOUT ISRAEL!..." "THEN NAOMI TOOK THE CHILD, LAID HIM IN HER LAP AND CARED FOR HIM. THE WOMEN LIVING THERE SAID, "NAOMI HAS A SON." AND THEY NAMED HIM OBED. HE WAS THE FATHER OF JESSE, THE FATHER OF DAVID."

MOTIVATIONAL MINUTE: DO NOT ALLOW YOURSELF TO DREAD TOMORROW. JUST KNOW THAT GOD IS FAITHFUL.

1 SAMUEL - ASKED OF GOD

HOW WAS SAMUEL'S BIRTH SPECIAL?

ANSWER:

A MAN NAMED ELKANAH HAD TWO WIVES CALLED HANNAH AND PENINNAH. PENINNAH HAD CHILDREN, BUT HANNAH COULD NOT. BECAUSE HANNAH COULD NOT HAVE CHILDREN, PENINNAH WOULD TEASE HER AND IRRITATE HER. SO HANNAH PRAYED TO GOD TO BLESS HER WITH A CHILD AND IF HE DID, SHE WOULD DEDICATE HIS LIFE BACK TO THE LORD. SO IN THE COURSE OF TIME, GOD BLESSED HER WITH A SON NAMED SAMUEL. GOD USED HIM TO DO HIS WILL, AS A PRIEST, FOR THE REST OF HIS LIFE.

SCRIPTURE REFERENCE: 1 SAMUEL 1:10-11, 27-28

"IN BITTERNESS OF SOUL HANNAH WEPT MUCH AND PRAYED TO THE LORD. AND SHE MADE A VOW, SAYING, "O LORD ALMIGHTY, IF YOU WILL ONLY LOOK UPON YOUR SERVANT'S MISERY AND REMEMBER ME, AND NOT FORGET YOUR SERVANT BUT GIVE HER A SON, THEN I WILL GIVE HIM TO THE LORD FOR ALL THE DAYS OF HIS LIFE, AND NO RAZOR WILL EVER BE USED ON HIS HEAD.".…"I PRAYED FOR THIS CHILD, AND THE LORD HAS GRANTED ME WHAT I ASKED OF HIM. SO NOW I GIVE HIM TO THE LORD. FOR HIS WHOLE LIFE HE WILL BE GIVEN OVER TO THE LORD.…."

MOTIVATIONAL MINUTE: WHENEVER YOU FEEL YOUR SPIRIT STARTING TO SINK, YOU NEED TO TAKE ACTION IMMEDIATELY. DON'T WAIT.

WHY DID GOD PUT A CURSE ON THE HOUSE OF ELI THE PRIEST?

ANSWER:

Eli was the priest who watched over Samuel as a boy. When Eli was old, his two sons, Hophni and Phinehas, were doing bad things in God's holy tent of meeting. This was considered a great sin against God. After Eli confronted them, they did not listen and continued to do wicked things. Because Eli did nothing to stop it, God sent a man to tell him that his family would be cursed and all of his descendants would die, because they disobeyed God. In addition to this, both of his sons would die on the same day, as another sign to Eli.

SCRIPTURE REFERENCE: 1 SAMUEL 2:29-34

"Why do you scorn my sacrifice and offering that I prescribed for my dwelling? Why do you honor your sons more than me by fattening yourselves on the choice parts of every offering made by my people Israel?" ..."Everyone of you that I do not cut off from my altar will be spared only to blind your eyes with tears and to grieve your heart, and all your descendants will die in the prime of life. And what happens to your two sons, Hophni and Phinehas, will be a sign to you - they will both die on the same day."

MOTIVATIONAL MINUTE: God has given you a heart of compassion, but you choose whether to open or close it.

WHY DID THE PEOPLE OF ISRAEL ASK FOR A KING?

Answer:

After Samuel had ruled over Israel for many years and grew old, he appointed his sons, Joel and Abijah as judges for Israel. But his sons were dishonest and took bribes. So the elders asked Samuel to appoint a king to lead them. This made Samuel sad, so he prayed to the Lord and asked him for direction. The Lord told Samuel to give the people what they wanted, because they weren't rejecting him but were rejecting God. And God wanted to warn them that the new king would cause them great pain.

Scripture Reference: 1 Samuel 8:4-9

"So all the elders of Israel gathered together and came to Samuel at Ramah. They said to him, "You are old, and your sons do not walk in your ways; now appoint a king to lead us, such as all the other nations have." ..."Now listen to them; but warn them solemnly and let them know what the king who will reign over them will do."

MOTIVATIONAL MINUTE: Before you respond to people too quickly, stop and listen to what the Holy Spirit has to say about your situation.

WHY DIDN'T SAUL WANT TO BE KING?

ANSWER:

God had revealed to Samuel that the new king would come from the Benjamin tribe. Saul and his servant went looking for his donkeys that were lost. When they couldn't find them, they wanted to see the priest to give them direction. Once Samuel saw Saul, God revealed to him that he was the chosen king. Samuel told Saul what God had revealed. Saul wasn't very happy because he thought he was unworthy. When Saul's uncle asked him what had happened to him after he returned home, he told his uncle about the lost donkeys being found, but not his appointed kingship of God.

SCRIPTURE REFERENCE: 1 Samuel 10:15-16, 23-24

"Saul's uncle said, "Tell me what Samuel said to you." Saul replied. "He assured us that the donkeys had been found." But he did not tell his uncle what Samuel had said about the kingship." ..."They ran and brought him out, and as he stood among the people he was a head taller than any of the others. Samuel said to all the people, "Do you see the man the Lord has chosen? There is no one like him among all the people." Then the people shouted. "Long live the king!"

MOTIVATIONAL MINUTE: Before you respond to people too quickly, stop and listen to what the Holy Spirit has to say about your situation.

HOW COULD THE LORD REJECT SAUL AS KING?

ANSWER:

SAMUEL TOLD SAUL THAT THE LORD WANTED HIM TO TOTALLY DESTROY ALL THE PEOPLE AND POSSESSIONS OF THE AMALEKITES BECAUSE OF THEIR EVIL DOINGS TO ISRAEL. BUT WHEN SAUL AND HIS ARMY DESTROYED THE AMALEKITES, THEY SAVED THEIR KING, AGAG, AND THE BEST LIVESTOCK AND POSSESSIONS, AS A SACRIFICE TO GOD. BUT GOD WAS ANGRY BECAUSE SAUL GAVE IN TO HIS PEOPLE AND DIDN'T OBEY HIM BY DESTROYING EVERYTHING. BECAUSE SAUL HAD REJECTED THE WORD OF GOD, GOD REJECTED HIM AS KING.

SCRIPTURE REFERENCE: 1 SAMUEL 15:17-26

"SAMUEL SAID, "ALTHOUGH YOU WERE ONCE SMALL IN YOUR EYES, DID YOU NOT BECOME THE HEAD OF THE TRIBES OF ISRAEL? THE LORD ANNOINTED YOU KING OVER ISRAEL. AND HE SENT YOU ON A MISSION, SAYING, GO AND COMPLETELY DESTROY THOSE WICKED PEOPLE, THE AMALEKITES; MAKE WAR ON THEM UNTIL YOU HAVE WIPED THEM OUT. WHY DID YOU NOT OBEY THE LORD? WHY DID YOU POUNCE ON THE PLUNDER AND DO EVIL IN THE EYES OF THE LORD?" ..."BUT SAMUEL SAID TO HIM, "I WILL NOT GO BACK WITH YOU. YOU HAVE REJECTED THE WORD OF THE LORD, AND THE LORD HAS REJECTED YOU AS KING OVER ISRAEL!"

MOTIVATIONAL MINUTE: THE FRUIT OF THE SPIRIT IS SELF-CONTROL, AND THE FRUIT OF THE FLESH IS NO CONTROL.

WHY DID DAVID'S HARP MAKE SAUL FEEL BETTER?

Answer:

After God rejected Saul as king, Samuel annointed David, the shepard boy from Bethlehem, to be king. Saul was unaware of this and became filled with evil spirits because God's spirit had left him. Saul's attendants had heard of David's ability to play the harp as well as being a brave man. So they asked David to play his harp for Saul in order for him to feel better. And when David agreed to play for him, the evil spirit would leave Saul's body and he would feel better.

Scripture Reference: 1 Samuel 16:15, 23

"Saul's attendants said to him, "See, an evil spirit from God is tormenting you. Let our Lord command his servants here to search for someone who can play the harp. He will play when the evil spirit from God comes upon you, and you will feel better." ..."Whenever the spirit from God came upon Saul. David would take his harp and play. Then relief would come to Saul; he would feel better, and the evil spirit would leave him.""

MOTIVATIONAL MINUTE: God has a plan for each of us, and the good things that happen to us are not just a coincidence.

HOW CAN A BOY KILL A GIANT WITH ONE STONE?

ANSWER:

THE PHILISTINES HAD GATHERED TOGETHER TO FIGHT KING SAUL AND THE ISRAELITES. GOLIATH WAS A NINE FOOT GIANT WHO WAS A PART OF THE PHILISTINE CAMP. HE TOLD THE ISRAELITES THAT IF ANY MAN WOULD FIGHT HIM AND WIN, THEN THE PHILISTINES WOULD BE THEIR SERVANTS. AND SAUL SAID IF ANYONE KILLED HIM, HE WOULD BECOME WEALTHY, WOULD GIVE HIS DAUGHTER IN MARRIAGE, AND WOULDN'T HAVE TO PAY TAXES. AND IF GOLIATH WON, THE ISRAELITES WOULD BE THEIR SERVANTS. DAVID BROUGHT FOOD TO HIS BROTHERS WHO WERE IN SAUL'S ARMY AND OVERHEARD WHAT GOLIATH HAD SAID. HE BECAME ANGRY AND TOLD SAUL THAT HE WOULD FIGHT HIM, BECAUSE GOD HAD HELPED HIM TO KILL LIONS AND BEARS WHEN HE WAS WATCHING OVER HIS FATHER'S SHEEP. SO INSTEAD OF WEARING A COAT OF ARMOR AND A HELMET, HE CHOSE FIVE SMOOTH STONES FROM A STREAM AND HIS SLINGSHOT. WHEN GOLIATH APPROACHED HIM AND LAUGHED, DAVID SHOT HIM IN THE HEAD WITH ONE STONE, IN THE NAME OF THE LORD. THE STONE SANK INTO HIS FOREHEAD, THEN HE DIED. WHEN THE PHILISTINES SAW THAT GOLIATH WAS DEAD, THEY RAN AWAY.

SCRIPTURE REFERENCE: 1 SAMUEL 17:40-50

"THEN HE TOOK HIS STAFF IN HIS HAND, CHOSE FIVE SMOOTH STONES FROM THE STREAM, PUT THEM IN THE POUCH OF HIS SHEPHERD'S BAG AND, WITH HIS SLING IN HIS HAND, APPROACHED THE PHILISTINE." ...."REACHING INTO HIS BAG AND TAKING OUT A STONE, HE SLUNG IT AND STRUCK THE PHILISTINE ON THE FOREHEAD. THE STONE SANK INTO HIS FOREHEAD, AND HE FELL FACEDOWN ON THE GROUND....."

MOTIVATIONAL MINUTE: JESUS SAID TO GO TO YOUR MOST PRIVATE ROOM WHEN YOU PRAY TO THE FATHER, AND HE WILL REWARD YOU OPENLY FOR THE TIME YOU SPEND WITH HIM.

WHY DID DAVID LIVE IN PHILISTINE ENEMY TERRITORY?

Answer:

BECAUSE SAUL WAS JEALOUS OF DAVID AND WANTED HIM DEAD, DAVID KNEW THAT IF HE LIVED IN PHILISTINE TERRITORY HIS LIFE WOULD BE SPARED AND SAUL WOULD GIVE UP. SO DAVID AND SIX HUNDRED OF HIS MEN, LIVED IN THE TOWN OF ZIKLAG FOR ONE YEAR AND FOUR MONTHS AS SERVANTS OF THE PHILISTINES UNTIL SAUL DIED.

SCRIPTURE REFERENCE: 1 SAMUEL 27:1-6

"BUT DAVID THOUGHT TO HIMSELF, "ONE OF THESE DAYS I WILL BE DESTROYED BY THE HAND OF SAUL. THE BEST THING I CAN DO IS TO ESCAPE TO THE LAND OF THE PHILISTINES. THEN SAUL WILL GIVE UP SEARCHING FOR ME ANYWHERE IN ISRAEL, AND I WILL SLIP OUT OF HIS HAND...." ...."SO ON THAT DAY ACHISH GAVE HIM ZIKLAG, AND IT HAS BELONGED TO THE KINGS OF JUDAH EVER SINCE. DAVID LIVED IN PHILISTINE TERRITORY A YEAR AND FOUR MONTHS."

MOTIVATIONAL MINUTE: YOU NEED TO LEARN NOT TO LET YOUR MIND AND EMOTIONS GET THE BEST OF YOU, ESPECIALLY WHEN IT INVOLVES THINGS OVER WHICH YOU HAVE NO CONTROL.

WHY DID SAUL ASK A WITCH FOR HELP?

ANSWER:

AFTER A PERIOD OF TIME, THE PRIEST, SAMUEL HAD DIED AND SAUL HAD MADE ALL OF THE MEDIUMS, WITCHES AND SPIRITISTS LEAVE THE LAND. THE PHILISTINES AND SAUL'S ARMY WERE ABOUT TO FIGHT AGAIN, SO SAUL PRAYED TO GOD FOR HELP. BUT GOD DID NOT ANSWER HIM, SO SAUL ASKED HIS ATTENDANTS TO FIND A MEDIUM OR WITCH FOR HIM TO CONSULT WITH. THEY FOUND A WITCH AND SAUL DISGUISED HIMSELF AND ASKED HER TO CONSULT A SPIRIT FOR HIM. THE WITCH WAS SCARED AND THOUGHT SHE WOULD BE KILLED, BUT SAUL TOLD HER IT WAS OK. SO THE WITCH, CALLED FOR SAMUEL'S SPIRIT AND HE CAME UP OUT OF THE GROUND. HE REVEALED TO SAUL THAT BECAUSE GOD HAD REJECTED HIM, HE WOULD DIE IN WAR THE NEXT DAY AND DAVID WOULD BE THE NEW KING OVER ISRAEL.

SCRIPTURE REFERENCE: 1 SAMUEL 28:3-19

"WHEN SAUL SAW THE PHILISTINE ARMY, HE WAS AFRAID; TERROR FILLED HIS HEART. HE INQUIRED OF THE LORD, BUT THE LORD DID NOT ANSWER HIM BY DREAMS OR URIM OR PROPHETS. SAUL THEN SAID TO HIS ATTENDANTS, "FIND ME A WOMAN WHO IS A MEDIUM, SO I MAY GO AND INQUIRE OF HER." ...."SAMUEL SAID, "WHY DO YOU CONSULT ME, NOW THAT THE LORD HAS TURNED AWAY FROM YOU AND BECOME YOUR ENEMY? THE LORD HAS DONE WHAT HE PREDICTED THROUGH ME. THE LORD HAS TORN THE KINGDOM OUT OF YOUR HANDS AND GIVEN IT TO ONE OF YOUR NEIGHBORS - TO DAVID...."

MOTIVATIONAL MINUTE: MANY PEOPLE DO NOT ENJOY PEACE BECAUSE THEY ARE OUT OF THE WILL OF GOD.

HOW COULD SAUL TAKE HIS OWN LIFE?

ANSWER:

AFTER SAMUEL'S SPIRIT REVEALED TO SAUL THAT HE WOULD DIE THE NEXT DAY, THE FIGHTING BETWEEN HIM AND THE PHILISTINES GREW FIERCE. THE PHILISTINES KILLED SAUL'S THREE SONS AND HAD WOUNDED HIM. SAUL DIDN'T WANT THE PHILISTINES TO HAVE THE SATISFACTION OF KILLING HIM, SO HE ASKED HIS ARMOR-BEARER TO KILL HIM WITH HIS SWORD. THE ARMOR-BEARER WAS SCARED, SO SAUL FELL ON HIS OWN SWORD AND KILLED HIMSELF AND THE ARMOR-BEARER DID THE SAME. SAUL, HIS THREE SONS AND HIS ARMOR-BEARER ALL DIED ON THE SAME DAY AS GOD HAD PREDICTED.

SCRIPTURE REFERENCE: 1 SAMUEL 31:1-6

".... THE PHILISTINES PRESSED HARD AFTER SAUL AND HIS SONS, AND THEY KILLED HIS SONS JONATHAN, ABINADAB AND MALKI-SHUA. THE FIGHTING GREW FIERCE AROUND SAUL, AND WHEN THE ARCHERS OVERTOOK HIM, THEY WOUNDED HIM CRITICALLY...."
"... BUT HIS ARMOR-BEARER WAS TERRIFIED AND WOULD NOT DO IT; SO SAUL TOOK HIS OWN SWORD AND FELL ON IT. WHEN THE ARMOR-BEARER SAW THAT SAUL WAS DEAD, HE TOO FELL ON HIS SWORD AND DIED WITH HIM...."

MOTIVATIONAL MINUTE: REFUSE TO ALLOW YOUR MIND, WILL, AND EMOTIONS TO RULE YOUR SPIRIT.

11 SAMUEL - ASKED OF GOD 2

WHY WAS DAVID ANOINTED KING OVER JUDAH?

Answer:

After David mourned Saul and Jonathan's death, the Lord told David to go to the town of Hebron to live. After he settled there with his two wives and his men, the men of Judah came to Hebron and anointed David king over the house of Judah. He reigned for seven years and six months.

Scripture Reference: 2 Samuel 2:1-4

"In the course of time, David inquired of the Lord. "Shall I go up to one of the towns of Judah?" he asked. The Lord said, "Go up." David asked, "Where shall I go?" "To Hebron," the Lord answered....." ...."Then the men of Judah came to Hebron and there they anointed David king over the house of Judah...."

Motivational Minute: Today is going to be a good day. Listen for the voice of God to lead you.

HOW DID DAVID BECOME KING OVER ISRAEL?

ANSWER:

AFTER YEARS OF FIGHTING BETWEEN THE HOUSE OF DAVID AND THE HOUSE OF SAUL, MANY OF SAUL'S DECENDENTS WERE KILLED. BECAUSE OF THIS, DAVID GREW STRONGER AND STRONGER, WHILE THE HOUSE OF SAUL GREW WEAKER AND WEAKER. ALL THE TRIBES OF ISRAEL CAME TO DAVID AND TOLD HIM THAT EVEN THOUGH SAUL WAS KING, HE WAS THE ONE WHO LED ISRAEL IN THEIR BATTLES. SO THE ELDERS OF ISRAEL AND DAVID MADE A COMPACT BEFORE THE LORD AND THEY MADE DAVID KING OVER ISRAEL.

SCRIPTURE REFERENCE: 2 SAMUEL 5:3

"WHEN ALL THE ELDERS OF ISRAEL HAD COME TO KING DAVID AT HEBRON, THE KING MADE A COMPACT WITH THEM AT HEBRON BEFORE THE LORD, AND THEY ANOINTED DAVID KING OVER ISRAEL."

MOTIVATIONAL MINUTE: TODAY CAN BE EFFORTLESS AS YOU DEPEND ON GOD'S GRACE TO DO WHAT HE HAS CALLED YOU TO DO.

WHY DID GOD MAKE A PROMISE TO DAVID?

ANSWER:

AFTER DAVID AND HIS MEN DEFEATED THE PHILISTINES, THE ARK OF GOD WAS BROUGHT FROM JUDAH TO ISRAEL. AFTER KING DAVID SETTLED IN HIS PALACE, HE SAID TO THE PROPHET NATHAN, THAT HE FELT BAD BECAUSE HE WAS LIVING IN A PALACE, WHILE THE ARK OF GOD WAS HOUSED IN A TENT. SO THAT NIGHT THE LORD SPOKE TO NATHAN AND TOLD HIM TO TELL DAVID THAT HE DIDN'T NEED TO DWELL IN A PALACE AND HE WOULD MAKE HIS NAME GREAT, LIKE THE NAMES OF THE GREATEST MEN OF THE EARTH. THE ISRAEL PEOPLE WOULD ALSO BE TAKEN CARE OF AND NO LONGER DISTURBED. GOD ALSO PROMISED THAT HE WOULD ALWAYS LOVE DAVID AND NOT TAKE IT AWAY LIKE HE DID SAUL. ADDITIONALLY, HIS THRONE AND KINGDOM WOULD BE ESTABLISHED FOREVER.

SCRIPTURE REFERENCE: 2 SAMUEL 7:2-16

"HE SAID TO NATHAN THE PROPHET, "HERE I AM, LIVING IN A PALACE OF CEDAR, WHILE THE ARK OF GOD REMAINS IN A TENT...." ...."THAT NIGHT THE WORD OF THE LORD CAME TO NATHAN, SAYING: "GO AND TELL MY SERVANT DAVID, "THIS IS WHAT THE LORD SAYS: ARE YOU THE ONE TO BUILD ME A HOUSE TO DWELL IN? I HAVE NOT DWELT IN A HOUSE FROM THE DAY I BROUGHT THE ISRAELITES UP OUT OF EGYPT TO THIS DAY. I HAVE BEEN MOVING FROM PLACE TO PLACE WITH A TENT AS MY DWELLING...." ...."BUT MY LOVE WILL NEVER BE TAKEN AWAY FROM HIM, AS I TOOK IT AWAY FROM SAUL, WHOM I REMOVED FROM BEFORE YOU...."

MOTIVATIONAL MINUTE: FOLLOW WHEREVER GOD LEADS YOU, AND DO WHATEVER HE TELLS YOU TO DO. YOU CAN EXPECT BETTER TOMORROWS WHEN YOU LIVE RIGHT TODAY.

WHY DID THE PROPHET NATHAN CURSE DAVID?

Answer:

During the spring, kings usually go off to war. David sent Joab and the Israelite army out to war and he stayed in Jerusalem. One evening David stood on his roof and saw a woman bathing, named Bathsheba. Bathsheba was very beautiful and was married to Uriah. David didn't care and slept with her anyway and she conceived a child. David sent for Uriah to come to the palace. He wanted him to go home and rest with his wife, but he refused to go home because he felt guilty that the other men were still fighting. So David told Joab to put him on the front line, were the fighting was the worst, so he would be killed. After Bathsheba mourned her husbands death, she became David's wife and had his son. The Lord was angry with David, so he sent the prophet Nathan to curse him. He told him that his son would die because he killed Uriah in order to have Bathsheba as his wife. And he would give all his other wives away.

Scripture Reference: 2 Samuel 12:7-16

".... Why did you despise the word of the Lord by doing what is evil in his eyes? You struck down Uriah the Hittite with the sword and took his wife to be your own. You killed him with the sword of the Ammonites. Now, therefore, the sword will never depart from your house, because you despised me and took the wife of Uriah the Hittite to be your own...." ...."Nathan replied, "The Lord has taken away your sin. You are not going to die. But because by doing this you have made the enemies of the Lord show utter contempt, the son born to you will die."...

MOTIVATIONAL MINUTE: Be responsible for your choices today. You cannot choose to live in the flesh and still expect everything to work out well.

WHY DID DAVID'S SON, ABSALOM, KILL HIS BROTHER AMNON?

Answer:

David's son Amnon fell in love with his beautiful sister, Tamar. Their brother Absalom, became angry with Amnon and tried to protect Tamar from him. But one night Amnon pretended he was sick and when Tamar brought him food, he raped her. Two years later, Absalom invited his father, King David, and his brothers to come to Baal Hazor to visit. David refused, so Absalom asked if his brother Amnon could come along with his other brothers. Once they arrived, Absalom ordered his men to kill Amnon while he was drinking wine. So the men did as they were told and killed Amnon as revenge of what he did to their sister, Tamar. Then Absalom ran away.

SCRIPTURE REFERENCE: 2 SAMUEL 13:28, 32

"Absalom ordered his men, "Listen! When Amnon is in high spirits from drinking wine and I say to you, "Strike Amnon down, then kill him. Don't be afraid. Have not I given you this order? Be strong and brave." "But Jonadab son of Shimeah, David's brother, said, "My lord should not think that they killed all the princes; only Amnon is dead. This has been Absalom's expressed intention ever since the day Amnon raped his sister Tamar."

MOTIVATIONAL MINUTE: Sometimes we come to an unhappy place in our lives. If we examine ourselves on those days, we will most likely discover that the things that make us most unhappy are the fruit of the choices that we made earlier.

HOW COME ABSALOM CONSPIRED AGAINST HIS FATHER DAVID?

Answer:

After Absalom returned to Jerusalem after three years, his father, King David, refused to see him. Two years had passed and David finally agreed to see him. In the course of time, Absalom started to become popular with the Israel people. He would stand at the kings gate and convince them that they needed a judge to hear their cases, because there wasn't a representative to hear them. After approximately four years, the people grew more fond of him. He then asked the king if he could worship God in the city of Hebron and the king agreed. Two hundred men went with Absalom as well as secret messengers of Israel. Absalom told the messengers to say, "Absalom is king in Hebron," when the trumpet sounded. And soon the conspiracy against the king increased and Absalom's following became stronger.

SCRIPTURE REFERENCE: 2 SAMUEL 15:1-12

"... And Absalom would add, "If only I were appointed judge in the land! Then everyone who has a complaint or case could come to me and I would see that he gets justice." ...."Then Absalom sent secret messengers throughout the tribes of Israel to say, "As soon as you hear the sound of the trumpets, then say, "Absalom is king in Hebron." Two hundred men from Jerusalem had accompanied Absalom. They had been invited as guests and went quite innocently, knowing nothing about the matter...."

MOTIVATIONAL MINUTE: If you want to keep peace, you can't always say everything you want to say. Sometimes you have to control yourself and apologize even when there is nothing in you that wants to do so.

WHY DID ABSALOM FIGHT AGAINST HIS FATHER, KING DAVID?

ANSWER:

A MESSENGER TOLD KING DAVID THAT THE ISRAEL PEOPLE APPROVED OF ABSALOM BEING KING. SO DAVID SET OUT TO PURSUE ABSALOM ALONG WITH SIX HUNDRED MEN. DAVID WAS VERY SAD BECAUSE HE DIDN'T WANT TO FIGHT HIS SON. BUT DAVID'S ADVISOR TO GOD, AHITHOPHEL, ADVISED ABSALOM TO DESPISE HIS FATHER, CHOOSE TWELVE THOUSAND MEN AND ATTACK HIM. HE ADVISED HIM TO ATTACK THE KING ONLY IN ORDER TO BRING ALL THE PEOPLE BACK TO HIM. THIS PLAN SEEMED GOOD TO ABSALOM AND TO ALL THE ELDERS OF ISRAEL. BUT ULTIMATELY ABSALOM DIED IN BATTLE.

SCRIPTURE REFERENCE: 2 SAMUEL 17:1-4

"AHITHOPHEL SAID TO ABSALOM, "I WOULD CHOOSE TWELVE THOUSAND MEN AND SET OUT TONIGHT IN PURSUIT OF DAVID. I WOULD ATTACK HIM WHILE HE IS WEARY AND WEAK. I WOULD STRIKE HIM WITH TERROR, AND THEN ALL THE PEOPLE WITH HIM WILL FLEE. I WOULD STRIKE DOWN ONLY THE KING AND BRING ALL THE PEOPLE BACK TO YOU. THE DEATH OF THE MAN YOU SEEK WILL MEAN THE RETURN OF ALL; ALL THE PEOPLE WILL BE UNHARMED." "THIS PLAN SEEMED GOOD TO ABSALOM AND TO ALL THE ELDERS OF ISRAEL."

MOTIVATIONAL MINUTE: SOME PEOPLE FIGHT WITH THE DEVIL ALL THE TIME, AND WHILE THEY ARE DOING SO, THEY ARE ALSO SPEAKING DEATH TO THEMSELVES AND THEIR SITUATION.

WHY DID ISRAEL HAVE FAMINE FOR THREE YEARS?

ANSWER:

DAVID ASKED THE LORD WHY ISRAEL HAD TO ENDURE FAMINE FOR THREE YEARS. THE LORD TOLD HIM THAT IT WAS BECAUSE OF KING SAUL PUTTING THE GIBEONITES, WHO WERE SURVIVORS OF THE AMORITES, TO DEATH. SO DAVID ASKED THE GIBEONITES WHAT HE COULD DO TO MAKE AMENDS. THEY ASKED IF SEVEN OF SAUL'S DESCENDANTS BE GIVEN TO THEM TO BE KILLED AND EXPOSED AT GIBEAH OF SAUL. DAVID AGREED AND AFTER THEY WERE PUT TO DEATH, GOD ANSWERED HIS PRAYER AND RELEASED THE FAMINE OF THE LAND.

SCRIPTURE REFERENCE: 2 SAMUEL 21:1, 5-6

"DURING THE REIGN OF DAVID, THERE WAS A FAMINE FOR THREE SUCCESSIVE YEARS; SO DAVID SOUGHT THE FACE OF THE LORD. THE LORD SAID, "IT IS ON ACCOUNT OF SAUL AND HIS BLOOD-STAINED HOUSE; IT IS BECAUSE HE PUT THE GIBEONITES TO DEATH."....."THEY ANSWERED THE KING, "AS FOR THE MAN WHO DESTROYED US AND PLOTTED AGAINST US SO THAT WE HAVE BEEN DECIMATED AND HAVE NO PLACE ANYWHERE IN ISRAEL, LET SEVEN OF HIS MALE DESCENDANTS BE GIVEN TO US TO BE KILLED AND EXPOSED BEFORE THE LORD AT GIBEAH OF SAUL - THE LORD'S CHOSEN ONE." SO THE KING SAID, "I WILL GIVE THEM TO YOU."

MOTIVATIONAL MINUTE: YOU KNOW GOD DOES NOT DO BAD THINGS. BUT SOMETIMES YOU MAY FAIL TO REALIZE THAT EVERYTHING THAT FEELS BAD TO YOU IS NOT NECESSARILY BAD FOR YOU.

HOW COME GOD GAVE DAVID THREE CHOICES OF PLAGUES ON ISRAEL?

Answer:

The Lord was angry with Israel, so He had David take a census of the fighting men of Israel and Judah. He sent Joab and the army of commanders out to count and at the end of nine months and twenty days, there were eight hundred thousand men in Israel and five hundred thousand in Judah. David felt guilty and begged the Lord to take away his guilt. So the next morning, Gad the prophet, told David that the Lord would give him three options of plagues. The choices were three years of famine, three months of pursuit from his enemies or three days of plague (death). David chose the plague on Israel and seventy thousand people died.

Scripture Reference: 2 Samuel 24:10-15

"David was conscience-stricken after he had counted the fighting men, and he said to the Lord, "I have sinned greatly in what I have done. Now, O Lord, I beg you, take away the guilt of your servant. I have done a very foolish thing." Before David got up the next morning, the word of the Lord had come to Gad the prophet, David's seer: "Go and tell David, this is what the Lord says: I am giving you three options. Choose one of them for me to carry out against you...."

MOTIVATIONAL MINUTE: Sometimes God asks us to do something. We usually wrestle with Him for a while and He allows us to rest awhile. And then He shows us something new that needs to be dealt with.

WHY DID DAVID HAVE TO BUILD GOD AN ALTAR?

ANSWER:

BECAUSE THE PLAGUE HAD ALREADY KILLED SEVENTY THOUSAND PEOPLE, DAVID WANTED IT TO STOP. HE ASKED THE LORD TO TAKE HIM AND HIS FAMILY INSTEAD. MEANWHILE, THE PLAGUE HAD CURRENTLY STOPPED AT THE HOUSE OF ARAUNAH, THE JEBUSITE. SO GAD THE PROPHET, TOLD DAVID TO BUILD AN ALTAR TO THE LORD ON THE HOUSE OF ARAUNAH. DAVID BOUGHT THE HOUSE, BUILT THE ALTAR AND SACRIFICED OFFERINGS. THEN THE LORD ANSWERED HIS PRAYER AND STOPPED THE PLAGUE ON ISRAEL.

SCRIPTURE REFERENCE: 2 SAMUEL 24:18-21, 25

"ON THAT DAY GAD WENT TO DAVID AND SAID TO HIM, "GO UP AND BUILD AN ALTAR TO THE LORD ON THE THRESHING FLOOR OF ARAUNAH THE JEBUSITE." SO DAVID WENT UP, AS THE LORD HAD COMMANDED THROUGH GAD."...."DAVID BUILT AN ALTAR TO THE LORD THERE AND SACRIFICED BURNT OFFERINGS AND FELLOWSHIP OFFERINGS. THEN THE LORD ANSWERED PRAYER IN BEHALF OF THE LAND, AND THE PLAGUE ON ISRAEL WAS STOPPED."

MOTIVATIONAL MINUTE: DON'T BECOME DISCOURAGED WITH YOURSELF WHEN YOU FALL SHORT. DON'T QUIT. KEEP AT IT UNTIL YOU HAVE DEVELOPED NEW HABITS.

1 KING - THE KINGDOM UNITED

WHY DID DAVID'S SON, ADONIJAH TRY TO BE THE NEW KING?

ANSWER:

WHEN KING DAVID BECAME SICK AND OLD, HIS SON, ADONIJAH, DECIDED THAT HE WOULD TAKE OVER AS KING. HE GOT CHARIOTS AND HORSES READY AND HAD FIFTY MEN RUN AHEAD OF HIM AS A SYMBOL. HE EVEN SACRIFICED SHEEP AND CATTLE AND INVITED ROYAL OFFICIALS, AND ALL HIS BROTHERS, EXCLUDING BROTHER SOLOMON, TO THE FEAST. ONCE KING DAVID FOUND OUT WHAT WAS HAPPENING, HE APPOINTED HIS SON, SOLOMON, AS THE NEW KING JUST AS HE PROMISED.

SCRIPTURE REFERENCE: 1 KING 1:5, 17-19, 30

"NOW ADONIJAH, WHOSE MOTHER WAS HAGGITH, PUT HIMSELF FORWARD AND SAID, "I WILL BE KING." SO HE GOT CHARIOTS AND HORSES READY, WITH FIFTY MEN TO RUN AHEAD OF HIM." …."SHE SAID TO HIM, "MY LORD, YOU YOURSELF SWORE TO ME YOUR SERVANT BY THE LORD YOUR GOD; SOLOMON YOUR SON SHALL BE KING AFTER ME, AND HE WILL SIT ON MY THRONE. BUT NOW ADONIJAH HAS BECOME KING, AND YOU, MY LORD THE KING, DO NOT KNOW ABOUT IT. HE HAS SACRIFICED GREAT NUMBERS OF CATTLE, FATTENED CALVES, AND SHEEP, AND HAS INVITED ALL THE KING'S SONS, ABIATHAR THE PRIEST AND JOAB THE COMMANDER OF THE ARMY, BUT HE HAS NOT INVITED SOLOMON YOUR SERVANT."…."I WILL SURELY CARRY OUT TODAY WHAT I SWORE TO YOU BY THE LORD, THE GOD OF ISRAEL: SOLOMON YOUR SON SHALL BE KING AFTER ME, AND HE WILL SIT ON MY THRONE IN MY PLACE."

MOTIVATIONAL MINUTE: WE DON'T ALWAYS WANT TO FACE TRUTH BECAUSE SOMETIMES IT IS PAINFUL. SOMETIMES IT SHOWS US THAT WE NEED TO CHANGE.

WHY DID KING SOLOMON KILL HIS BROTHER ADONIJAH?

ANSWER:

AFTER SOLOMON BECAME KING, HIS BROTHER, ADONIJAH, THOUGHT HE WOULD BE KILLED. BUT SOLOMON PROMISED NOT TO KILL HIM AS LONG AS HE DID NO EVIL. SO ADONIJAH ASKED SOLOMON'S MOTHER, BATHSHEBA, TO ASK SOLOMON IF HE COULD MARRY ABISHAG, THE SHUNAMMITE, WHO TOOK CARE OF THEIR FATHER, KING DAVID, WHEN HE WAS DYING. KING SOLOMON BECAME VERY ANGRY AND THOUGHT THAT HE MIGHT AS WELL ASK FOR THE KINGDOM ALSO. BECAUSE OF THIS EVIL REQUEST, SOLOMON HAD HIS BROTHER KILLED.

SCRIPTURE REFERENCE: 1 KING 2:22-25

"KING SOLOMON ANSWERED HIS MOTHER, "WHY DO YOU REQUEST ABISHAG THE SHUNAMMITE FOR ADONIJAH? YOU MIGHT AS WELL REQUEST THE KINGDOM FOR HIM - AFTER ALL, HE IS MY OLDER BROTHER - YES, FOR HIM AND FOR ABIATHAR THE PRIEST AND JOAB SON OF ZERUIAH!" ...."SO KING SOLOMON GAVE ORDERS TO BENAIAH SON OF JEHOIADA, AND HE STRUCK DOWN ADONIJAH AND HE DIED."

MOTIVATIONAL MINUTE: WHEN YOU TALK TO GOD, BE SURE TO ASK FOR FORGIVENESS OF YOUR SINS.

HOW COME GOD GAVE KING SOLOMON GREAT WISDOM?

ANSWER:

SOLOMON MADE AN ALLIANCE WITH PHAROAH, THE KING OF EGYPT, AND MARRIED HIS DAUGHTER. HE CONTINUED TO WORSHIP AND BELIEVE IN GOD LIKE HIS FATHER, DAVID. THE LORD CAME TO SOLOMON IN A DREAM AND TOLD HIM TO ASK FOR WHATEVER HE WANTED. SO SOLOMON ASKED FOR WISDOM, BECAUSE HE BELIEVED THAT HE NEEDED TO LEARN HOW TO CARRY OUT HIS DUTIES TO HIS PEOPLE. AND BECAUSE HE DIDN'T ASK FOR RICHES OR DEATH OF HIS ENEMIES, GOD GAVE HIM GREAT WISDOM AND RICHES THAT HE DIDN'T ASK FOR, AS LONG AS HE OBEYED AND KEPT GOD'S COMMANDS.

SCRIPTURE REFERENCE: 1 KING 3:9-12

"SO GIVE YOUR SERVANT A DISCERNING HEART TO GOVERN YOUR PEOPLE AND TO DISTINGUISH BETWEEN RIGHT AND WRONG. FOR WHO IS ABLE TO GOVERN THIS GREAT PEOPLE OF YOURS?" "THE LORD WAS PLEASED THAT SOLOMON HAD ASKED FOR THIS. SO GOD SAID TO HIM, "SINCE YOU HAVE ASKED FOR THIS AND NOT FOR LONG LIFE OR WEALTH FOR YOURSELF, NOR HAVE ASKED FOR THE DEATH OF YOUR ENEMIES BUT FOR DISCERNMENT IN ADMINISTERING JUSTICE, I WILL DO WHAT YOU HAVE ASKED. I WILL GIVE YOU A WISE AND DISCERNING HEART, SO THAT THERE WILL NEVER HAVE BEEN ANYONE LIKE YOU, NOR WILL THERE EVER BE."

MOTIVATIONAL MINUTE: ASK GOD TO SHOW YOU THE NEEDS OF PEOPLE THROUGH THE EYES OF JESUS TODAY. AND YOUR DAYS WILL NEVER BE WASTED.

WHY WAS SOLOMON GOING TO CUT A BABY IN HALF?

Answer:

Their were two prostitutes who lived with each other. They both had babies who were born three days apart. During the night, one of the babies died because one woman laid on him by mistake. So she took the other woman's baby instead and gave her dead baby to the other. When they awoke the next morning, the other woman knew that the babies had been switched. So they went to Solomon to decide who would keep the living baby. Solomon said he couldn't decide, so he would cut the baby in half. And as he was about to do this, the woman who's son was alive begged to give the baby to the other woman. But the other woman said to cut him in two. Because of her compassion, Solomon gave the baby to the first woman, because he knew she was his real mother.

Scripture Reference: 1 King 3:24-27

"Then the king said, "Bring me a sword." "So they brought a sword for the king. He then gave an order: "Cut the living child in two and give half to one and half to the other." The woman whose son was alive was filled with compassion for her son and said to the king, "Please, my Lord, give her the living baby! Don't kill him!" But the other said, "Neither I nor you shall have him. Cut him in two!" "Then the king gave his ruling: "Give the living baby to the first woman. Do not kill him; she is his mother."

Motivational Minute: God's word says He will provide protection and deliverance to all who put their faith and trust in Him.

WHY DID IT TAKE SOLOMON THIRTEEN YEARS TO BUILD HIS PALACE?

Answer:

After Solomon kept his promise to his father, David, that he would build a temple to God first, he then built his palace. It took him thirteen years to complete, because it was the largest and most detailed palace of its' time. It was made with the best wood, high-grade stone and pure gold.

Scripture Reference: 1 King 7:1-12

"It took Solomon thirteen years, however, to complete the construction of his palace." He built the palace of the forest of Lebanon a hundred cubits long, fifty wide and thirty high, with four rows of cedar columns supporting trimmed cedar beams..."

Motivational Minute: Do whatever the Lord puts in your heart to do- and enjoy fulfilling your God-given purpose.

HOW CAN SOLOMON HAVE SEVEN HUNDRED WIVES?

Answer:

King Solomon loved many foreign women, besides Pharoah's daughter. God told the Israelites not to marry them, because they worshipped other gods. But Solomon loved them anyway and eventually had seven hundred wives. As he grew old, Solomon began to worship other gods and he was not fully devoted to the Lord. And because of this, God became angry and told Solomon that He would take his kingdom from him, except one tribe, and give it to one of his subordinates. He would do so after his death, because his father, King David, was obedient to God.

Scripture Reference: 1 King 11:1-3, 9-13

"King Solomon, however, loved many foreign women besides Pharaoh's daughter - Moabites, Ammonites, Edomites, Sidonians and Hittites. They were from nations about which the Lord had told the Israelites. "You must not intermarry with them, because they will surely turn your hearts after their gods." Nevertheless, Solomon held fast to them in love He had seven hundred wives of royal birth and three hundred concubines, and his wives led him astray."....."So the Lord said to Solomon, "Since this is your attitude and you have not kept my covenant and my decrees, which I commanded you, I will most certainly tear the kingdom away from you and give it to one of your subordinates..."

MOTIVATIONAL MINUTE: God measures holiness by how quick we are to obey His voice. He promises that goodness and mercy will follow us if we seek His presence.

HOW DID ONE OF SOLOMON'S OFFICIALS BECOME KING?

ANSWER:

A MAN NAMED JEROBOAM WAS ONE OF SOLOMON'S OFFICIALS. HE WAS PUT IN CHARGE OF THE WHOLE LABOR FORCE. AHIJAH, THE PROPHET OF SHILOH, MET JEROBOAM AS HE WAS GOING OUT OF JERUSALEM AND GAVE HIM TEN PIECES OF HIS NEW ROBE. HE TOLD HIM THAT THE LORD WAS GOING TO TAKE TEN TRIBES AWAY FROM SOLOMON AND HIS SON, AND GIVE THEM TO HIM, BECAUSE OF SOLOMON'S DISOBEDIENCE. HE THEN FLED TO EGYPT UNTIL SOLOMON DIED. AND WHEN HE RETURNED, SOLOMON'S SON, REHOBOAM, WAS KING UNTIL THE ISRAELITES REJECTED HIM AND APPOINTED JEROBOAM, KING AS GOD PROMISED.

SCRIPTURE REFERENCE: 1 KING 11:27-41

"…..NOW JEROBOAM WAS A MAN OF STANDING, AND WHEN SOLOMON SAW HOW WELL THE YOUNG MAN DID HIS WORK, HE PUT HIM IN CHARGE OF THE WHOLE LABOR FORCE OF THE HOUSE OF JOSEPH. ABOUT THAT TIME JEROBOAM WAS GOING OUT OF JERUSALEM, AND AHIJAH THE PROPHET OF SHILOH MET HIM ON THE WAY, WEARING A NEW CLOAK. THE TWO OF THEM WERE ALONE OUT IN THE COUNTRY, AND AHIJAH TOOK HOLD OF THE NEW CLOAK HE WAS WEARING AND TORE IT INTO TWELVE PIECES. THEN HE SAID TO JEROBOAM, "TAKE TEN PIECES FOR YOURSELF, FOR THIS IS WHAT THE LORD, THE GOD OF ISRAEL, SAYS: "SEE, I AM GOING TO TEAR THE KINGDOM OUT OF SOLOMON'S HAND AND GIVE YOU TEN TRIBES…." …."SOLOMON TRIED TO KILL JEROBOAM, BUT JEROBOAM FLED TO EGYPT, TO SHISHAK THE KING, AND STAYED THERE UNTIL SOLOMON'S DEATH….."

MOTIVATIONAL MINUTE: GOD'S WAYS ARE NOT OUR WAYS, SO LEARN TO LISTEN FOR HIS DIRECTION EACH DAY.

HOW CAN A MAN BE FED BY RAVENS?

Answer:

All of the kings after Jeroboam continued to do evil and not keep God's commands. A prophet, named Elijah in Gilead, said to the latest King Ahab, of Israel, that there would be no dew or rain in the next few years. Then God told Elijah to go to the Kerith Ravine, east of the Jordan, and drink water from the brook. God also ordered the ravens (birds) to bring him bread and meat in the morning and evening until the brook dried up.

SCRIPTURE REFERENCE: 1 KING 17:1-5

"Now Elijah the Tishbite, from Tishbe in Gilead, said to Ahab, "As the Lord, the God of Israel, lives, whom I serve, there will be neither dew nor rain in the next few years except at my word." Then the word of the Lord came to Elijah: "Leave here, turn eastward and hide in the Kerith Ravine, east of the Jordan. You will drink from the brook, and I have ordered the ravens to feed you there." So he did what the Lord had told him. He went to the Kerith Ravine, east of the Jordan, and stayed there. The ravens brought him bread and meat in the morning and bread and meat in the evening, and he drank from the brook."

MOTIVATIONAL MINUTE: As a child of God, you need to know how to be steady and stable no matter what the circumstances. Allow His peace to guide your heart and mind, so you are prepared to handle times of crisis when they come.

HOW DID ELIJAH BRING THE WIDOW'S SON BACK TO LIFE?

ANSWER:

AFTER ELIJAH LEFT THE BROOK, GOD TOLD HIM TO GO TO ZAREPHATH AND STAY WITH A WIDOW FOR FOOD AND SHELTER. SHE TOLD HIM THAT SHE HAD NO BREAD, ONLY A HANDFUL OF FLOUR IN A JAR AND A LITTLE OIL IN A JUG. BUT ELIJAH TOLD HER THE LORD WOULD KEEP THE JAR OF FLOUR FULL AND THE OIL WOULD NOT DRY UP UNTIL IT RAINED. AFTER THAT, THE SON OF THE WOMAN BECAME ILL AND STOPPED BREATHING. SHE BLAMED ELIJAH AND ACCUSED HIM OF TRYING TO KILL HER SON, BECAUSE OF HER SIN. SO ELIJAH TOOK HIM TO THE UPPER ROOM, PRAYED AND STRETCHED OUT OVER HIM THREE TIMES AND ASKED GOD TO BRING THE BOY BACK TO LIFE. AND BECAUSE THE BOY LIVED, THE WOMAN WAS CONVINCED THAT HE WAS A MAN OF GOD.

SCRIPTURE REFERENCE: 1 KING 17:14-24

"FOR THIS IS WHAT THE LORD, THE GOD OF ISRAEL, SAYS: "THE JAR OF FLOUR WILL NOT BE USED UP AND THE JUG OF OIL WILL NOT RUN DRY UNTIL THE DAY THE LORD GIVES RAIN ON THE LAND." ...."SOME TIME LATER THE SON OF THE WOMAN WHO OWNED THE HOUSE BECAME ILL. HE GREW WORSE AND WORSE, AND FINALLY STOPPED BREATHING. SHE SAID TO ELIJAH, "WHAT DO YOU HAVE AGAINST ME, MAN OF GOD? DID YOU COME TO REMIND ME OF MY SIN AND KILL MY SON?" "GIVE ME YOUR SON," ELIJAH REPLIED. HE TOOK HIM FROM HER ARMS, CARRIED HIM TO THE UPPER ROOM WHERE HE WAS STAYING, AND LAID HIM ON HIS BED. THEN HE CRIED OUT TO THE LORD, "O LORD MY GOD, HAVE YOU BROUGHT TRAGEDY ALSO UPON THIS WIDOW I AM STAYING WITH, BY CAUSING HER SON TO DIE?" THEN HE STRETCHED HIMSELF OUT ON THE BOY THREE TIMES AND CRIED TO THE LORD, "O LORD MY GOD, LET THIS BOY'S LIFE RETURN TO HIM!" THE LORD HEARD ELIJAH'S CRY, AND THE BOY'S LIFE RETURNED TO HIM, AND HE LIVED...."

MOTIVATIONAL MINUTE: WHEN YOU TRUST GOD, YOU DON'T HAVE TO BE AFRAID OF THE DEVILS SUDDEN SURPRISES THAT STALK YOU. HE IS YOUR STRONG FORTRESS.

HOW DID KING AHAB DIE FROM A STRAY BOW AND ARROW?

ANSWER:

KING AHAB AND KING ARAM WENT TO RAMOTH GILEAD TO FIGHT IN BATTLE OVER THIS LAND. AHAB DISGUISED HIMSELF, BUT TOLD JEHOSHAPHAT, KING OF JUDAH, TO WEAR HIS ROYAL ROBES. KING ARAM'S MEN WENT TO ATTACK JEHOSHAPHAT, BUT HE CRIED OUT AND THEY STOPPED PURSUING HIM. BUT SOMEONE DREW A STRAY BOW AND ARROW AT RANDOM, AND IT STRUCK KING AHAB BETWEEN HIS ARMOR. THAT NIGHT HE DIED.

SCRIPTURE REFERENCE: 1 KING 22:29-35

"SO THE KING OF ISRAEL AND JEHOSHAPHAT KING OF JUDAH WENT UP TO RAMOTH GILEAD. THE KING OF ISRAEL SAID TO JEHOSHAPHAT, "I WILL ENTER THE BATTLE IN DISGUISE, BUT YOU WEAR YOUR ROYAL ROBES." SO THE KING OF ISRAEL DISGUISED HIMSELF AND WENT INTO BATTLE...." ...."SO THEY TURNED TO ATTACK HIM, BUT WHEN JEHOSHAPHAT CRIED OUT, THE CHARIOT COMMANDERS SAW THAT HE WAS NOT THE KING OF ISRAEL AND STOPPED PURSUING HIM. BUT SOMEONE DREW HIS BOW AT RANDOM AND HIT THE KING OF ISRAEL BETWEEN THE SECTIONS OF HIS ARMOR. THE KING TOLD HIS CHARIOT DRIVER, "WHEEL AROUND AND GET ME OUT OF THE FIGHTING, I'VE BEEN WOUNDED."...."THE BLOOD FROM HIS WOUND RAN ONTO THE FLOOR OF THE CHARIOT, AND THAT EVENING HE DIED."

MOTIVATIONAL MINUTE: GOD REQUIRES US TO TRUST HIM AND TRUST REQUIRES UNANSWERED QUESTIONS.

11 KING - THE KINGDOM DIVIDED

HOW DID ELIJAH GO TO HEAVEN IN A TORNADOE?

ANSWER:

The prophets, Elijah and Elisha, were on their way from Gilgal and God told Elijah to go to Bethel. Elisha didn't want Elijah to go by himself so he went also. And when they arrived, the company of the prophets told Elisha that God was going to take Elijah from him that day. Elisha knew this was going to happen, but didn't want to acknowledge it. So they walked on to Jericho and Jordan, and the same thing was said again. Once they got to the Jordan River, Elijah rolled up his coat and struck the water with it. The water then divided to the right and left, so they could cross over on dry land. Elijah then asked Elisha what he could do for him before he was taken away. And Elisha asked for a double portion of his spirit. Then a chariot and horses of fire appeared, and Elijah went up to heaven in a whirlwind, like a tornadoe. Then the Lord gave Elisha, Elijah's spirit as he requested.

SCRIPTURE REFERENCE: 2 KING 2:11

"As they were walking along and talking together, suddenly a chariot of fire and horses of fire appeared and separated the two of them, and Elijah went up to heaven in a whirlwind."

MOTIVATIONAL MINUTE: Ask God to fill you with power of self-control in order to overcome procrastination and be a doer of the word.

HOW DID THE SHUNAMMITE BOY COME BACK FROM THE DEAD?

Answer:

THE PROPHET ELISHA, WAS STAYING IN A CITY CALLED SHUNEM. AND WHENEVER HE WENT THERE, A SHUNAMMITE WOMAN WOULD FEED HIM. BECAUSE SHE KNEW HE WAS A MAN OF GOD, HER AND HER HUSBAND SET UP A ROOM FOR HIM TO STAY WHENEVER HE CAME TO TOWN. BECAUSE THEY WERE NICE TO HIM, ELISHA TOLD THEM THAT THEY WOULD HAVE A SON NEXT YEAR. SHE DIDN'T BELIEVE HIM BECAUSE HER HUSBAND WAS OLD. BUT AT THAT SAME TIME THE FOLLOWING YEAR, SHE HAD A SON. ONE DAY THE SON COMPLAINED ABOUT HIS HEAD AND DIED WHILE SITTING IN HIS MOTHER'S LAP. SHE THEN LAID HIM ON ELISHA'S BED AND SHUT THE DOOR. SHE LEFT AND FOUND ELISHA AT MOUNT CARMEL AND HE IMMEDIATELY WENT TO HER HOME. HE LAID DOWN ON TOP OF THE BOY, MOUTH TO MOUTH, EYES TO EYES, HANDS TO HANDS, AND THE BOY'S BODY BECAME WARM. THEN AFTER SNEEZING SEVEN TIMES, THE BOY OPENED HIS EYES AND WAS ALIVE AGAIN.

SCRIPTURE REFERENCE: 2 KING 4:32-36

"WHEN ELISHA REACHED THE HOUSE, THERE WAS THE BOY LYING DEAD ON HIS COUCH. HE WENT IN, SHUT THE DOOR ON THE TWO OF THEM AND PRAYED TO THE LORD. THEN HE GOT ON THE BED AND LAY UPON THE BOY, MOUTH TO MOUTH, EYES TO EYES, HANDS TO HANDS. AS HE STRETCHED HIMSELF OUT UPON HIM, THE BOY'S BODY GREW WARM. ELISHA TURNED AWAY AND WALKED BACK AND FORTH IN THE ROOM AND THEN GOT ON THE BED AND STRETCHED OUT UPON HIM ONCE MORE. THE BOY SNEEZED SEVEN TIMES AND OPENED HIS EYES. ELISHA SUMMONED GEHAZI AND SAID, "CALL THE SHUNAMMITE." AND HE DID. WHEN SHE CAME, HE SAID, "TAKE YOUR SON.""

MOTIVATIONAL MINUTE: SPENDING TIME WITH GOD WILL FILL YOU WITH "LIVING WATER." YOU WILL BE EDIFIED AND BECOME A SOURCE OF ENCOURAGEMENT FOR OTHERS ALL DAY LONG.

HOW CAN A HUNDRED PEOPLE EAT WITH TWENTY LOAVES OF BREAD?

ANSWER:

A MAN CAME TO ELISHA WITH TWENTY LOAVES OF BARLEY BREAD ALONG WITH GRAIN. ELISHA TOLD THE MAN TO GIVE IT TO THE HUNDRED PEOPLE TO EAT. THE MAN DID NOT BELIEVE THAT HIS BREAD WOULD FEED THIS MANY PEOPLE, SO ELISHA TOLD HIM THAT GOD SAID TO GIVE IT TO THEM. THE MAN DID WHAT HE WAS TOLD AND THE PEOPLE ATE THE BREAD AND HAD SOME LEFT OVER, JUST AS GOD SAID.

SCRIPTURE REFERENCE: 2 KING 4:42-44

"A MAN CAME FROM BAAL SHALISHAH, BRINGING THE MAN OF GOD TWENTY LOAVES OF BARLEY BREAD BAKED FROM THE FIRST RIPE GRAIN, ALONG WITH SOME HEADS OF NEW GRAIN. "GIVE IT TO THE PEOPLE TO EAT," ELISHA SAID. "HOW CAN I SET THIS BEFORE A HUNDRED MEN?" HIS SERVANT ASKED. BUT ELISHA ANSWERED, "GIVE IT TO THE PEOPLE TO EAT, FOR THIS IS WHAT THE LORD SAYS: THEY WILL EAT AND HAVE SOME LEFT OVER." "THEN HE SET IT BEFORE THEM, AND THEY ATE AND HAD SOME LEFT OVER, ACCORDING TO THE WORD OF THE LORD."

MOTIVATIONAL MINUTE: GIVE THANKS FOR WHAT YOU HAVE, WITHOUT LOOKING AT WHAT YOU DON'T HAVE.

WHY DID HAZAEL MURDER HIS MASTER, KING BEN-HADAD?

Answer:

When Ben-Hadad was king of Aram, he became ill. When the prophet Elisha went to Damascus, the king sent Hazael there to meet him and ask if he would recover. Elisha told Hazael that the king would survive his illness, but he would kill him and become king of Aram. When Hazael returned home, he told Ben-Hadad that he would recover, but the next day he suffocated him and the king died.

Scripture Reference: 2 King 8:10-13

"Elisha answered, "Go and say to him, you will certainly recover: but the Lord has revealed to me that he will in fact die." ...."Hazael said, "How could your servant, a mere dog, accomplish such a feat?" "The Lord has shown me that you will become king of Aram," answered Elisha."

MOTIVATIONAL MINUTE: If there is anything between us and God, when we try to pray and get into His presence, it will bother us until we deal honestly with it.

HOW CAN JOASH BECOME KING AT SEVEN YEARS OLD?

Answer:

AFTER AHAZIAH, THE KING OF JUDAH WAS KILLED, HIS MOTHER ATHALIAH, TRIED TO KILL THE WHOLE ROYAL FAMILY, IN ORDER TO RULE THE LAND. AHAZIAH'S SISTER TOOK HIS SON, JOASH, AND HID HIM AND HIS NURSE FOR SIX YEARS. IN THE SEVENTH YEAR, JEHOIADA, THE PRIEST, BROUGHT OUT JOASH AND PUT A CROWN ON HIM AND PROCLAIMED HIM AS KING. WHEN ATHALIAH FOUND OUT, SHE WAS CAPTURED AND JEHOIADA ORDERED THE COMMANDERS TO PUT HER TO DEATH. JEHOIADA THEN MADE A COVENANT BETWEEN GOD AND THE KING THAT THEY WOULD BE THE LORD'S PEOPLE. JOASH WAS SEVEN YEARS OLD WHEN HE BEGAN TO REIGN.

SCRIPTURE REFERENCE: 2 KING 11:2-3, 12, 21

"BUT JEHOSHEBA, THE DAUGHTER OF KING JEHORAM AND SISTER OF AHAZIAH, TOOK JOASH SON OF AHAZIAH AND STOLE HIM AWAY FROM AMONG THE ROYAL PRINCES, WHO WERE ABOUT TO BE MURDERED. SHE PUT HIM AND HIS NURSE IN A BEDROOM TO HIDE HIM FROM ATHALIAH; SO HE WAS NOT KILLED. HE REMAINED HIDDEN WITH HIS NURSE AT THE TEMPLE OF THE LORD FOR SIX YEARS WHILE ATHALIAH RULED THE LAND." "JEHOIADA BROUGHT OUT THE KING'S SON AND PUT THE CROWN ON HIM; HE PRESENTED HIM WITH A COPY OF THE COVENANT AND PROCLAIMED HIM KING. THEY ANOINTED HIM, AND THE PEOPLE CLAPPED THEIR HANDS AND SHOUTED, "LONG LIVE THE KING!" "JOASH WAS SEVEN YEARS OLD WHEN HE BEGAN TO REIGN."

MOTIVATIONAL MINUTE: YOU SHOULD HAVE YOUR MIND RENEWED TO WHAT LOVE REALLY IS.

WHY DID GOD TAKE THE ISRAELITES FROM THEIR HOMELAND?

Answer:

All the kings who reigned in Israel sinned against God. Because of this, the Israelites followed their kings and also continued to sin against God. After Hosea, which was the last king of Israel ruled, Shalmaneser, king of Assyria, captured him and deported the Israelites to Assyria. God allowed this to happen, because the Israelites didn't follow God's commands, by worshipping idols and practicing divination and sorcery. And because of God's anger with Israel, he rejected and removed them from his presence.

Scripture Reference: 2 King 17:6, 16-23

"In the ninth year of Hoshea, the king of Assyria captured Samaria and deported the Israelites to Assyria. He settled them in Halah, in Gozan on the Habor river and in the towns of the Medes."....."So the Lord was very angry with Israel and removed them from his presence. Only the tribe of Judah was left, and even Judah did not keep the commands of the Lord their God. They followed the practices Israel had introduced. Therefore the Lord rejected all the people of Israel; he afflicted them and gave them into the hands of plunderers, until he thrust them from his presence." ...."So the people of Israel were taken from their homeland into exile in Assyria, and they are still there."

Motivational Minute: God wants us to abide in Him, not just visit Him occasionally.

WHY DID GOD GIVE KING HEZEKIAH FIFTEEN MORE YEARS TO LIVE?

ANSWER:

King Hezekiah became ill, and was told by the prophet Isaiah, that he would die. Hezekiah prayed to God asking to spare his life, because he had been faithful and done good in his eyes. God heard his prayer, and told the prophet to tell Hezekiah that he would recover and live another fifteen years, as well as defeat the new king of Assyria.

SCRIPTURE REFERENCE: 2 KING 20:1-6

"In those days Hezekiah became ill and was at the point of death. The prophet Isaiah son of Amoz went to him and said, "This is what the Lord says; put your house in order, because you are going to die; you will not recover." ...."Go back and tell Hezekiah, the leader of my people, this is what the Lord, the God of your father David, says: I have heard your prayer and seen your tears; I will heal you. On the third day from now you will go up to the temple of the Lord. I will add fifteen years to your life. And I will deliver you and this city from the hand of the king of Assyria. I will defend this city for my sake and for the sake of my servant David."

MOTIVATIONAL MINUTE: What a great high priest we have in Jesus. He understands our experiences, and He knows what it is like to live in a human body.

HOW CAN THE ANGEL OF THE LORD KILL A HUNDRED AND EIGHTY-FIVE THOUSAND ASSYRIAN MEN?

ANSWER:

Sennacherib, the king of Assyria, threatened to fight Hezekiah, the king of Judah. He sent messengers to Hezekiah reporting that he shouldn't depend on God to defeat him, because he had destroyed all of the other kings in the past. When Hezekiah received the message, he took it to God and asked God for guidance and protection. God heard his prayer and promised him that Judah would be saved and King Sennacherib would not enter his city at all. So that night the angel of the Lord put to death a hundred and eighty-five thousand Assyrian men. And the king of Assyria withdrew his army and never returned. One day when Sennacherib was worshipping his god Nisroch, his two sons killed him with a sword.

SCRIPTURE REFERENCE: 2 KING 19:35-36

"That night the angel of the Lord went out and put to death a hundred and eighty-five thousand men in the Assyrian camp. When the people got up the next morning - there were all dead bodies! So Sennacherib king of Assyria broke camp and withdrew. He returned to Nineveh and stayed there."

MOTIVATIONAL MINUTE: Ask God to put into your spirit everything He wants you to know.

HOW WAS TH BOOK OF THE LAW FOUND?

ANSWER:

WHEN THE NEW KING, JOSIAH OF JERUSALEM, WAS EIGHTEEN YEARS OLD, HE HAD THE TEMPLE OF GOD REPAIRED. HE WAS DEDICATED TO DOING THE WORK OF THE LORD. THE HIGH PRIEST TOLD THE SECRETARY THAT HE FOUND THE BOOK OF THE LAW IN THE TEMPLE. AFTER THE SECRETARY READ IT, HE TOOK IT TO KING JOSIAH AND READ IT TO HIM. WHEN THE KING HEARD GOD'S LAW, HE BECAME UPSET AND VOWED TO DO HIS WILL, BECAUSE HIS FOREFATHERS HAD NOT OBEYED THE LAW. THE KING SENT THE MEN TO SPEAK WITH PROPHETESS HULDAH. SHE TOLD THEM THAT GOD WAS ANGRY, AND HE WOULD BRING DISASTER TO THEM, BECAUSE THE LAWS WERE BROKEN. BUT BECAUSE KING JOSIAH HAD HUMBLED HIMSELF, AND BURNED ALL THE IDOLS THAT WERE MADE, GOD FORGAVE THEM AND DIDN'T BRING DISASTER TO THEM.

SCRIPTURE REFERENCE: 2 KING 22:8-20

"HILKIAH THE HIGH PRIEST SAID TO SHAPHAN THE SECRETARY, "I HAVE FOUND THE BOOK OF THE LAW IN THE TEMPLE OF THE LORD." HE GAVE IT TO SHAPHAN, WHO READ IT. THEN SHAPHAN THE SECRETARY WENT TO THE KING AND REPORTED TO HIM: "YOUR OFFICIALS HAVE PAID OUT THE MONEY THAT WAS IN THE TEMPLE OF THE LORD AND HAVE ENTRUSTED IT TO THE WORKERS AND SUPERVISORS AT THE TEMPLE." THEN SHAPHAN THE SECRETARY INFORMED THE KING. "HILKIAH THE PRIEST HAS GIVEN ME A BOOK." AND SHAPHAN READ FROM IT IN THE PRESENCE OF THE KING." ...."SHE SAID TO THEM, "THIS IS WHAT THE LORD, THE GOD OF ISRAEL, SAYS: TELL THE MAN WHO SENT YOU TO ME, THIS IS WHAT THE LORD SAYS: I AM GOING TO BRING DISASTER ON THIS PLACE AND ITS PEOPLE, ACCORDING TO EVERYTHING WRITTEN IN THE BOOK THE KING OF JUDAH HAS READ." ...."BECAUSE YOUR HEART WAS RESPONSIVE AND YOU HUMBLED YOURSELF BEFORE THE LORD WHEN YOU HEARD WHAT I HAVE SPOKEN AGAINST THIS PLACE AND ITS PEOPLE, THAT THEY WOULD BE ACCURSED AND LAID WASTE, AND BECAUSE YOU TORE YOUR ROBES AND WEPT IN MY PRESENCE, I HAVE HEARD YOU, DECLARES THE LORD. THEREFORE I WILL GATHER YOU TO YOUR FATHERS, AND YOU WILL BE BURIED IN PEACE. YOUR EYES WILL NOT SEE ALL THE DISASTER I AM GOING TO BRING ON THIS PLACE."

MOTIVATIONAL MINUTE: "LORD, PLEASE HELP ME TO CHANGE. SHOW ME THE ROOT OF MY PROBLEM AND HOW TO GET OVER IT. I WANT POSITIVE CHANGES IN MY LIFE."

WHY DID GOD ALLOW JERUSALEM TO BE CAPTURED?

Answer:

When King Josiah's son, Zedekiah, from Jerusalem reigned, he continued to do evil, just like his forefathers had done. God became very angry and allowed King Nebuchadnezzar of Babylon, to take over and destroy Jerusalem. After the Babylonian army captured the people, they killed Zedekiah's sons in front of him, and took him to Babylon to be killed. Then they set fire to the temple of the Lord, the palace, and all the houses of Jerusalem. It was because of God's anger that all this happened to Jerusalem and Judah. So the people went into captivity, away from their land.

Scripture Reference: 2 King 25:1-21

"Now Zedekiah rebelled against the king of Babylon. So in the ninth year of Zedekiah's reign, on the tenth day of the tenth month, Nebuchadnezzar king of Babylon marched against Jerusalem with his whole army. He encamped outside the city and built siege works all around it." ...."And he was captured. He was taken to the king of Babylon at Riblah, where sentence was pronounced on him. They killed the sons of Zedekiah before his eyes. Then they put out his eyes, bound him with bronze shackles and took him to Babylon." ...."There at Riblah, in the land of Hamath, the king had them executed. So Judah went into captivity, away from her land."

MOTIVATIONAL MINUTE: You should judge yourself soberly, knowing that without God you can do nothing of value.

1 CHRONICLES - WORDS OF THE DAYS

WHAT IS A GATEKEEPER?

ANSWER:

In Jerusalem, the Levite gatekeepers were people who were stationed at the King's gate on the east. And the Korahite people were responsible for guarding the doors of the temple. Altogether, there was a total of two hundred and twelve. The gatekeepers were also in charge of guarding the gates of the house of God and were stationed on all four sides: east, west, north and south. The Levites were also responsible for the rooms and treasuries in the house of God.

SCRIPTURE REFERENCE: 1 CHRONICLES 9:17-34

"Altogether, those chosen to be gatekeepers at the thresholds numbered 212. They were registered by genealogy in their villages. The gatekeepers had been assigned to their positions of trust by David and Samuel the seer. They and their descendants were in charge of guarding the gates of the house of the Lord - the house called the tent. The gatekeepers were on the four sides: east, west, north and south..." ...."But the four principal gatekeepers, who were Levites, were entrusted with the responsibility for the rooms and treasuries in the house of God....."

MOTIVATIONAL MINUTE: Waiting on God purifies your faith and builds character in you.

WHY DID GOD HAVE THE LEVITES BRING UP THE "ARK OF THE LORD" TO JERUSALEM?

ANSWER:

King David prepared a tent or palace for the ark, after he constructed buildings for himself in the city of David. The Lord chose the Levites to carry the ark of God, in order to minister before Him forever. Because the Levites did not bring the ark to its' place the first time, the Lord was angry with them. So after the Levites consecrated themselves, they carried the ark of God to Jerusalem, just as God commanded before to Moses.

SCRIPTURE REFERENCE: 1 CHRONICLES 15:2, 11-15

"Then David said, "No one but the Levites may carry the ark of God, because the Lord chose them to carry the ark of the Lord and to minister before Him forever...." ...."It was because you, the Levites, did not bring it up the first time that the Lord our God broke out in anger against us. We did not inquire of Him about how to do it in the prescribed way." "So the priests and Levites consecrated themselves in order to bring up the ark of the Lord, the God of Israel. And the Levites carried the ark of God with the poles on their shoulders, as Moses had commanded in accordance with the word of the Lord."

MOTIVATIONAL MINUTE: There will be no "bad day" when God's word supports, strengthens, and directs us.

WHY DID KING SAUL HAVE TO DIE?

Answer:

The Philistines fought against Israel, in which many were killed. The Philistines killed Saul's sons and injured him. Because Saul's armor-bearer was scared and didn't want to kill him with his sword, Saul fell on his own sword and took his own life. Saul died because he was unfaithful to God and consulted a medium (witch) for guidance, instead of God. And because of this, God turned the kingdom over to David.

Scripture Reference: 1 Chronicles 10:1-6, 13

"....The fighting grew fierce around Saul, and when the archers overtook him, they wounded him. Saul said to his armor-bearer, "Draw your sword and run me through, or these uncircumcised fellows will come and abuse me." "But his armor-bearer was terrified and would not do it; so Saul took his own sword and fell on it...." ...."Saul died because he was unfaithful to the Lord; he did not keep the word of the Lord and even consulted a medium for guidance, and did not inquire of the Lord. So the Lord put him to death and turned the kingdom over to David son of Jesse."

Motivational Minute: By focusing on the goodness of God and waiting, hoping, and expecting Him to encourage you and fill you with His peace and joy, you can overcome negative thoughts that drag you down.

HOW COME DAVID WANTED HIS SON, SOLOMON, TO BUILD A TEMPLE FOR THE LORD?

Answer:

After King David had fought and won wars and also sinned against God, he wanted to build a temple for God. While he was beginning to assemble his people, God told him to let his son, Solomon, build his temple. He wanted Solomon to do this, because of David's great bloodshed in war. God said that Solomon would be a man of peace and he would rest from his enemies. And when Solomon became king, after David's death, God would continue to grant peace during his reign.

Scripture Reference: 1 Chronicles 22:6-10

"Then he called for his son Solomon and charged him to build a house for the Lord, the God of Israel. David said to Solomon: "My son, I had it in my heart to build a house for the Name of the Lord my God. But this word of the Lord came to me: You have shed much blood and have fought many wars, you are not to build a house for my Name, because you have shed much blood on the earth in my sight. But you will have a son who will be a man of peace and rest, and I will give him rest from all his enemies on every side. His name will be Solomon, and I will grant Israel peace and quiet during his reign. He is the one who will build a house for my Name. He will be my son, and I will be his father. And I will establish the throne of his kingdom over Israel forever.""

MOTIVATIONAL MINUTE: We should be so hungry for the presence of God, that we absolutely will not go out of our house or tackle any kind of project, until we have spent some time with God.

WHY DID DAVID PRAY IN FRONT OF EVERYONE?

ANSWER:

AFTER KING DAVID WAS BLESSED WITH HAVING THE BEST RESOURCES TO BUILD THE TEMPLE, HE WANTED TO THANK GOD AND REJOICE IN FRONT OF THE WHOLE ASSEMBLY OF GOD. HE WANTED TO ACKNOWLEDGE THAT HE AND THE ISRAEL PEOPLE WASN'T WORTHY OF GOD'S BLESSINGS. EVERYTHING THEY HAD WAS GIVEN TO THEM BY GOD. HE PRAISED GOD BY RETURNING GOD'S BLESSINGS AND RESOURCES, BACK TO HIM. AND TO GIVE HIS SON, SOLOMON, THE COMMAND TO KEEP GOD'S PROMISES AND DECREES TO BUILD THE TEMPLE THAT HE PROVIDED.

SCRIPTURE REFERENCE: 1 CHRONICLES 29:10-20

"DAVID PRAISED THE LORD IN THE PRESENCE OF THE WHOLE ASSEMBLY, SAYING, "PRAISE BE TO YOU, O LORD, GOD OF OUR FATHER ISRAEL, FROM EVERLASTING TO EVERLASTING. YOURS, O LORD, IS THE GREATNESS AND THE POWER AND THE GLORY AND THE MAJESTY AND THE SPLENDOR, FOR EVERYTHING IN HEAVEN AND EARTH IS YOURS. YOURS, O LORD, IS THE KINGDOM; YOU ARE EXALTED AS HEAD OVER ALL. WEALTH AND HONOR COME FROM YOU; YOU ARE THE RULER OF ALL THINGS. IN YOUR HANDS ARE STRENGTH AND POWER TO EXALT AND GIVE STRENGTH TO ALL. NOW, OUR GOD, WE GIVE YOU THANKS, AND PRAISE YOUR GLORIOUS NAME...."

MOTIVATIONAL MINUTE: MANY BELIEVERS SERVE GOD WITH THEIR TIME, BUT STILL MISS SPENDING PERSONAL TIME IN HIS PRESENCE.

11 CHRONICLES - WORDS OF THE DAYS CONTINUED

HOW CAN GOD TURN INTO A DARK CLOUD?

Answer:

After King Solomon built the temple of God and brought the ark back to the temple, he gave thanks. The Levites were accompanied by 120 priests and played instruments and sang to God. Then God filled the temple with a dark cloud and the priests couldn't continue their service, because of the cloud. Solomon told them that God would live in the dark cloud as a place to live forever.

Scripture Reference: 2 Chronicles 5:13-14, 6:1-2

"The trumpeters and singers joined in unison, as with one voice, to give praise and thanks to the Lord. Accompanied by trumpets, cymbals and other instruments, they raised their voices in praise to the Lord and sang: "He is good; his love endures forever." Then the temple of the Lord was filled with a cloud, and the priests could not perform their service because of the cloud, for the glory of the Lord filled the temple of God. Then Solomon said, "The Lord has said that he would dwell in a dark cloud; I have built a magnificent temple for you, a place for you to dwell forever."

MOTIVATIONAL MINUTE: Jesus will actually dwell, settle down, abide, and make His permanent home in your heart!

WHY DID GOD APPEAR TO SOLOMON?

Answer:

After Solomon had finished dedicating the temple of the Lord and building the palace, God appeared to him at night. God told Solomon that He had heard his prayer and had chosen to live in the temple for sacrifices. He also told Solomon that if the people sinned and He turned away from them, as long as they humbled themselves and repented of their sins, He would heal their land. If Solomon continued to obey God's laws and decrees, then he would continue to rule over Israel as well as his family. But if he turned away from God and worshipped other gods, then He would reject the Israel people and the temple He blessed.

Scripture Reference: 2 Chronicles 7:12-22

"The Lord appeared to him at night and said: "I have heard your prayer and have chosen this place for myself as a temple for sacrifices. When I shut up the heavens so that there is no rain, or command locusts to devour the land or send a plague among my people, if my people, who are called by my name, will humble themselves and pray and seek my face and turn from their wicked ways, then will I hear from heaven and will forgive their sin and will heal their land...." ...."As for you, if you walk before me as David your father did, and do all I command, and observe my decrees and laws, I will establish your royal throne, as I covenanted with David your father when I said, You shall never fail to have a man to rule over Israel. But if you turn away and forsake the decrees and commands I have given you and go off to serve other gods and worship them, then I will uproot Israel from my land, which I have given them, and will reject this temple I have consecrated for my Name..."

Motivational Minute: Repent in the morning to enjoy God's mercy, forgiveness, and love all day.

WHY DID THE QUEEN OF SHEBA GIVE KING SOLOMON GIFTS?

ANSWER:

THE QUEEN OF SHEBA HAD HEARD A LOT ABOUT KING SOLOMON AND HIS FAME. SHE WANTED TO TEST HIS WISDOM BY ASKING VERY HARD QUESTIONS. SHE ALSO BROUGHT HIM SPICES, LARGE AMOUNTS OF GOLD AND PRECIOUS STONES. BECAUSE OF SOLOMON'S GREAT WISDOM, HE WAS ABLE TO ANSWER ALL OF SHEBA'S QUESTIONS. SHE WAS SO IMPRESSED BY HIM, AND THE PALACE HE HAD BUILT, THAT SHE GAVE HIM ALL OF THE GIFTS THAT SHE BROUGHT. THERE HAD NEVER BEEN SUCH GIFTS AS THOSE THE QUEEN OF SHEBA BROUGHT TO KING SOLOMON.

SCRIPTURE REFERENCE: 2 CHRONICLES 9:1-4

"WHEN THE QUEEN OF SHEBA HEARD OF SOLOMON'S FAME, SHE CAME TO JERUSALEM TO TEST HIM WITH HARD QUESTIONS. ARRIVING WITH A VERY GREAT CARAVAN- WITH CAMELS CARRYING SPICES, LARGE QUANTITIES OF GOLD, AND PRECIOUS STONES- SHE CAME TO SOLOMON AND TALKED WITH HIM ABOUT ALL SHE HAD ON HER MIND. SOLOMON ANSWERED ALL HER QUESTIONS; NOTHING WAS TOO HARD FOR HIM TO EXPLAIN TO HER. WHEN THE QUEEN OF SHEBA SAW THE WISDOM OF SOLOMON, AS WELL AS THE PALACE HE HAD BUILT, THE FOOD ON HIS TABLE, THE SEATING OF HIS OFFICIALS, THE ATTENDING SERVANTS IN THEIR ROBES, THE CUPBEARERS IN THEIR ROBES AND THE BURNT OFFERINGS HE MADE AT THE TEMPLE OF THE LORD, SHE WAS OVERWHELMED."

MOTIVATIONAL MINUTE: YOU WILL GET JOYFUL WHEN YOU BEGIN TO THINK ABOUT HOW YOU CAN BLESS SOMEBODY ELSE.

WHY DID ASA, THE KING OF JUDAH, REFORM HIMSELF?

Answer:

When King Asa became king, he did good in the eyes of the Lord. He removed idols and altars and smashed sacred stones. And commanded that Judah seek the Lord also. Because of this, the Lord gave Asa ten years of peace from war. A prophet named Azariah, spoke to Asa and said that the Lord was with him, as long as he continued to believe and worship him, and against him if he didn't. He told him to be strong and not give up, because his work would be rewarded. After Asa heard everything, he removed all of the idols from the whole land of Judah, Benjamin, and all the towns he captured in Ephraim. He also repaired the altar in front of the Lord's temple. Because Asa did this, there was no war for thirty-five years.

Scripture Reference: 2 Chronicles 15:1-8

"The Spirit of God came upon Azariah son of Oded. He went out to meet Asa and said to him, "Listen to me, Asa and all Judah and Benjamin. The Lord is with you when you are with Him. If you seek Him, He will be found by you, but if you forsake Him, He will forsake you. For a long time Israel was without the true God, without a priest to teach and without the law...."
...."When Asa heard these words and the prophecy of Azariah son of Oded the prophet, he took courage. He removed the detestable idols from the whole land of Judah and Benjamin and from the towns he had captured in the hills of Ephraim. He repaired the altar of the Lord that was in front of the portico of the Lord's temple."

Motivational Minute: Seek God with your whole heart today. Talk to Him about your problems, and then enjoy yourself, knowing that He cares for you.

HOW DID KING JEHOSHAPHAT DEFEAT THE MOABITES AND AMMONITES?

ANSWER:

AFTER KING JEHOSHAPHAT OF JUDAH, HEARD THAT THE MOABITES AND AMMONITES WANTED TO DEFEAT HIM IN WAR, HE DECLARED A FAST FOR ALL THE PEOPLE AND PRAYED TO GOD. HE PRAYED THAT GOD WOULD SAVE THEM FROM THESE ENEMIES, BECAUSE THEY WANTED TO DRIVE HIM OUT OF HIS LAND GOD PROMISED. THE SPIRIT OF THE LORD SPOKE THROUGH JAHAZIEL, A LEVITE, AND TOLD THEM NOT TO BE AFRAID OR DISCOURAGED. HE TOLD THEM THAT THEY DIDN'T HAVE TO FIGHT THIS BATTLE, AND TO STAND FIRM BECAUSE THE LORD WOULD BE WITH THEM. AFTER THE PEOPLE HEARD THIS, THEY BEGAN TO SING AND PRAISE THE LORD. AND WHEN THEY WENT TO DEFEAT THE MOABITES AND AMMONITES, THEY WERE AMBUSHED AND ALREADY DEAD, JUST AS GOD PROMISED.

SCRIPTURE REFERENCE: 2 CHRONICLES 20:1-30

"AFTER THIS, THE MOABITES AND AMMONITES WITH SOME OF THE MEUNITES CAME TO MAKE WAR ON JEHOSHAPHAT. SOME MEN CAME AND TOLD JEHOSHAPHAT, "A VAST ARMY IS COMING AGAINST YOU FROM EDOM, FROM THE OTHER SIDE OF THE SEA. IT IS ALREADY IN HAZAZON TAMAR" (THAT IS, EN GEDI). ALARMED, JEHOSHAPHAT RESOLVED TO INQUIRE OF THE LORD, AND HE PROCLAIMED A FAST FOR ALL JUDAH. THE PEOPLE OF JUDAH CAME TOGETHER TO SEEK HELP FROM THE LORD; INDEED, THEY CAME FROM EVERY TOWN IN JUDAH TO SEEK HIM...." ...."THEN THE SPIRIT OF THE LORD CAME UPON JAHAZIEL SON OF ZECHARIAH, THE SON OF BENAIAH, THE SON OF JEIEL, THE SON OF MATTANIAH, A LEVITE AND DESCENDANT OF ASAPH, AS HE STOOD IN THE ASSEMBLY. HE SAID: "LISTEN, KING JEHOSHAPHAT AND ALL WHO LIVE IN JUDAH AND JERUSALEM! THIS IS WHAT THE LORD SAYS TO YOU; 'DO NOT BE AFRAID OR DISCOURAGED BECAUSE OF THIS VAST ARMY. FOR THE BATTLE IS NOT YOURS, BUT GOD'S...." ...."WHEN THE MEN OF JUDAH CAME TO THE PLACE THAT OVERLOOKS THE DESERT AND LOOKED TOWARD THE VAST ARMY, THEY SAW ONLY DEAD BODIES LYING ON THE GROUND; NO ONE HAD ESCAPED...."

MOTIVATIONAL MINUTE: GOD KNOWS WHAT WE WANT AND WHAT WE NEED. HE WANTS TO GIVE US BLESSINGS THAT WE HAVEN'T EVEN VERBALLY ASKED FOR.

EZRA - BORN IN CONFUSION

WHY DID CYRUS, THE KING OF PERSIA, HELP THE PEOPLE RETURN TO JERUSALEM?

Answer:

After the messenger, Jeremiah, predicted from God that the people would be captured by Nebuchadnezzar of Babylon for seventy years, God moved the heart of Cyrus King of Persia, to rebuild a temple for Him. He proclaimed in writing that God gave him all the kingdoms. If any of the people believed in God, they could bring their prized possessions to the temple as offerings to God. So the family heads, the priests and Levites, left Babylon to rebuild God's temple in Jerusalem, as God had said.

Scripture Reference: Ezra 1:1-5

"In the first year of Cyrus king of Persia, in order to fulfill the word of the Lord spoken by Jeremiah, the Lord moved the heart of Cyrus king of Persia to make a proclamation throughout his realm and to put it in writing: "This is what Cyrus king of Persia says: "The Lord, the God of heaven, has given me all the kingdoms of the earth and he has appointed me to build a temple for him at Jerusalem in Judah...." ...."Then the family heads of Judah and Benjamin, and the priests and Levites - everyone whose heart God had moved - prepared to go up and build the house of the Lord in Jerusalem."

Motivational Minute: If we aren't living the way God has instructed us to live, we will be miserable until we confess our sins. Once we thoroughly get everything out in the open before the Lord, He gives us the power to be set free.

WHY DID PEOPLE OPPOSE THE REBUILDING OF THE TEMPLE?

ANSWER:

THE ENEMIES OF THE PEOPLE OF JERUSALEM WANTED TO HELP THEM REBUILD THE TEMPLE OF GOD. THE HEADS OF THE FAMILIES REFUSED, BECAUSE THEY WANTED TO REBUILD IT ALONE, JUST AS KING CYRUS HAD COMMANDED THEM. BECAUSE OF THIS, THE ENEMIES SENT MESSENGERS TO DISCOURAGE THE PEOPLE TO CONTINUE BUILDING THE TEMPLE.

SCRIPTURE REFERENCE: EZRA 4:1-4

"WHEN THE ENEMIES OF JUDAH AND BENJAMIN HEARD THAT THE EXILES WERE BUILDING A TEMPLE FOR THE LORD, THE GOD OF ISRAEL, THEY CAME TO ZERUBBABEL AND TO THE HEADS OF THE FAMILIES AND SAID, "LET US HELP YOU BUILD BECAUSE, LIKE YOU, WE SEEK YOUR GOD AND HAVE BEEN SACRIFICING TO HIM SINCE THE TIME OF ESARHADDON KING OF ASSYRIA, WHO BROUGHT US HERE." BUT ZERUBBABEL, JESHUA AND THE REST OF THE HEADS OF THE FAMILIES OF ISRAEL ANSWERED, "YOU HAVE NO PART WITH US IN BUILDING A TEMPLE TO OUR GOD. WE ALONE WILL BUILD IT FOR THE LORD, THE GOD OF ISRAEL, AS KING CYRUS, THE KING OF PERSIA, COMMANDED US." THEN THE PEOPLES AROUND THEM SET OUT TO DISCOURAGE THE PEOPLE OF JUDAH AND MAKE THEM AFRAID TO GO ON BUILDING."

MOTIVATIONAL MINUTE: IF YOU NEED ENCOURAGEMENT, SPEND TIME WITH SOMEONE WHO KNOWS HOW TO BUILD YOU UP. DON'T IGNORE YOUR EMOTIONAL NEEDS IN THE NAME OF CHRISTIANITY.

WHY DID KING ARTAXERXES OF BABYLON, LET EZRA TAKE ALL THE ISRAELITES BACK TO JERUSALEM?

Answer:

Ezra was a priest and a teacher in the Law of Moses. He lived in Babylon and traveled back to Jerusalem as most Israelites were doing. Because Ezra was a priest of God, King Artaxerxes trusted him and allowed all of the Israelites who lived in Babylon to go back with him to Jerusalem. Artaxerxes also allowed it, because God had placed it in his heart and had blessed him and his officials.

Scripture Reference: Ezra 7:6-13

"This Ezra came up from Babylon. He was a teacher well versed in the Law of Moses, which the Lord, the God of Israel, had given. The king had granted him everything he asked, for the hand of the Lord his God was on him. Some of the Israelites, including priests, Levites, singers, gatekeepers and temple servants, also came up to Jerusalem in the seventh year of King Artaxerxes...." ...."Artaxerxes, king of kings, to Ezra the priest, a teacher of the Law of the God of heaven: Greetings. Now I decree that any of the Israelites in my kingdom, including priests and Levites, who wish to go to Jerusalem with you, may go."

Motivational Minute: As you get to know God better, you will undergo a transition from just praying during times of trouble to wanting to serve Him with everything you are, every breath you take, and every talent you possess.

HOW DID THE TEMPLE FINALLY GET COMPLETED?

ANSWER:

AFTER THE ENEMIES OPPOSED THE REBUILDING OF THE TEMPLE, THEY SENT A LETTER TO KING ARTAXERXES OF PERSIA TO STOP CONSTRUCTION. THE CONSTRUCTION CAME TO A STANDSTILL UNTIL THE SECOND YEAR THAT DARIUS BECAME KING OF PERSIA. AFTER KING DARIUS FOUND THE ORDER THAT WAS ISSUED BY KING CYRUS TO RESTORE GOD'S TEMPLE, HE TOLD THE GOVERNOR OF TRANS-EUPHRATES TO CARRY IT OUT. AND THE PEOPLE FINISHED THE TEMPLE AS GOD COMMANDED IN SIX YEARS.

SCRIPTURE REFERENCE: EZRA 6:13-15

"THEN, BECAUSE OF THE DECREE KING DARIUS HAD SENT, TATTENAI, GOVERNOR OF TRANS-EUPHRATES, AND SHETHAR-BOZENAI AND THEIR ASSOCIATES CARRIED IT OUT WITH DILIGENCE. SO THE ELDERS OF THE JEWS CONTINUED TO BUILD AND PROSPER UNDER THE PREACHING OF HAGGAI THE PROPHET AND ZECHARIAH, A DESCENDANT OF IDDO. THEY FINISHED BUILDING THE TEMPLE ACCORDING TO THE COMMAND OF THE GOD OF ISRAEL AND THE DECREES OF CYRUS, DARIUS AND ARTAXERXES, KINGS OF PERSIA. THE TEMPLE WAS COMPLETED ON THE THIRD DAY OF THE MONTH ADAR, IN THE SIXTH YEAR OF THE REIGN OF KING DARIUS."

MOTIVATIONAL MINUTE: ENJOY THE ABUNDANT LIFE THAT JESUS CHRIST DESIRES FOR YOU TO HAVE. THE DEVIL WILL ALWAYS TRY TO SET YOU UP TO GET UPSET.

WHY WAS EZRA ANGRY ABOUT SOME OF THE ISRAELITE MARRIAGES?

Answer:

After the people returned to Jerusalem, the leaders told Ezra that some of the people had married men and women from the surrounding cities that God didn't approve of. God's command was for them not to be friends or marry people who practiced evil and was corrupted. Because the people married anyway, Ezra prayed to God for forgiveness. The Israelites confessed of their sin, and removed the foreign people from Jerusalem, in order to do God's will.

Scripture Reference: Ezra 9:1-6, 10:2-3

"After these things had been done, the leaders came to me and said, "The people of Israel, including the priests and the Levites, have not kept themselves separate from the neighboring peoples with their detestable practices, like those of the Canaanites, Hittites, Perizzites, Jebusites, Ammonites, Moabites, Egyptians and Amorites. They have taken some of their daughters as wives for themselves and their sons, and have mingled the holy race with the peoples around them. And the leaders and officials have led the way in this unfaithfulness....." ....."Then Shecaniah son of Jehiel, one of the descendants of Elam, said to Ezra, "We have been unfaithful to our God by marrying foreign women from the peoples around us. But in spite of this, there is still hope for Israel. Now let us make a covenant before our God to send away all these women and their children, in accordance with the counsel of my lord and of those who fear the commands of our God. Let it be done according to the law."

MOTIVATIONAL MINUTE: The Bible contains guidelines for a good life. It is not a book of laws; it is about liberty and freedom to live the life that reaps good things.

NEHEMIAH – COMFORTER OF GOD

WHY DID NEHEMIAH WANT TO REBUILD THE WALL OF JERUSALEM?

ANSWER:

AFTER THE ISRAELITES CAME BACK TO JERUSALEM, NEHEMIAH'S BROTHER, HANANI, TOLD HIM THAT THE PEOPLE WERE UPSET, BECAUSE THE WALL OF JERUSALEM WAS BROKEN DOWN, AND THE GATES WERE BURNED. NEHEMIAH WAS SAD AND PRAYED TO GOD FOR AN ANSWER. AND BECAUSE HE WAS A CUPBEARER TO KING ARTAXERXES, HE ASKED THE KING IF HE COULD GO TO JERUSALEM TO REBUILD THE WALL. KING ARTAXERXES GRANTED HIS REQUEST.

SCRIPTURE REFERENCE: NEHEMIAH 2:3-6

"BUT I SAID TO THE KING, "MAY THE KING LIVE FOREVER! WHY SHOULD MY FACE NOT LOOK SAD WHEN THE CITY WHERE MY FATHERS ARE BURIED LIES IN RUINS, AND ITS GATES HAVE BEEN DESTROYED BY FIRE?" THE KING SAID TO ME, "WHAT IS IT YOU WANT?" THEN THE KING, WITH THE QUEEN SITTING BESIDE HIM, ASKED ME, "HOW LONG WILL YOUR JOURNEY TAKE, AND WHEN WILL YOU GET BACK?" IT PLEASED THE KING TO SEND ME; SO I SET A TIME."

MOTIVATIONAL MINUTE: A TRULY DISCIPLINED PERSON HAS THE ABILITY TO SUBORDINATE THE LESSER CHOICE TO THE GREATER, MORE EXCELLENT CHOICE. THINK ABOUT THAT, AS YOU CHOOSE THE WAY YOU WILL GO TODAY.

WHY DID SANBALLAT AND TOBIAH OPPOSE REBUILDING THE WALL?

ANSWER:

AFTER SANBALLAT AND TOBIAH, THE ARABS AND AMMONITES, HEARD THAT THE JERUSALEM WALL WAS BEING REBUILT, THEY BECAME VERY ANGRY. THEY TALKED ABOUT THE ISRAELITES, AND SAID THEY WOULD NEVER BE ABLE TO REBUILD THE WALL, AND IT WOULD BE WEAK. THEY ALSO PRAYED TO THEIR GOD TO MAKE THEM WEAK, AND TO HAVE BAD THINGS HAPPEN TO THEM. WHEN THE ISRAELITES CONTINUED TO REBUILD, SANBALLAT AND TOBIAH PLOTTED TO FIGHT AGAINST THEM. BUT THE ISRAELITES PRAYED TO GOD AND POSTED GUARDS DAY AND NIGHT FOR PROTECTION.

SCRIPTURE REFERENCE: NEHEMIAH 4:1-9

"WHEN SANBALLAT HEARD THAT WE WERE REBUILDING THE WALL, HE BECAME ANGRY AND WAS GREATLY INCENSED. HE RIDICULED THE JEWS, AND IN THE PRESENCE OF HIS ASSOCIATES AND THE ARMY OF SAMARIA, HE SAID, "WHAT ARE THOSE FEEBLE JEWS DOING? WILL THEY RESTORE THEIR WALL? WILL THEY OFFER SACRIFICES? WILL THEY FINISH IN A DAY? CAN THEY BRING THE STONES BACK TO LIFE FROM THOSE HEAPS OF RUBBLE - BURNED AS THEY ARE?" TOBIAH THE AMMONITE, WHO WAS AT HIS SIDE, SAID, "WHAT THEY ARE BUILDING - IF EVEN A FOX CLIMBED UP ON IT, HE WOULD BREAK DOWN THEIR WALL OF STONES!....." ....."THEY ALL PLOTTED TOGETHER TO COME AND FIGHT AGAINST JERUSALEM AND STIR UP TROUBLE AGAINST IT. BUT WE PRAYED TO OUR GOD AND POSTED A GUARD DAY AND NIGHT TO MEET THIS THREAT."

MOTIVATIONAL MINUTE: WE NEED TO BE SO SELF-CONTROLLED THAT WE DON'T WASTE TIME.

WHY DID THE ISRAELITES CRY WHEN EZRA READ THE BOOK OF THE LAW?

ANSWER:

AFTER THE WALL OF JERUSALEM WAS COMPLETED AND EVERYONE WAS SETTLED, EZRA THE PRIEST, READ THE BOOK OF THE LAW TO THE PEOPLE. AS HE READ, THE PEOPLE BEGAN TO GRIEVE AND CRY. NEHEMIAH TOLD THEM NOT TO CRY, BUT TO CELEBRATE, BECAUSE THEY FINALLY UNDERSTOOD GOD'S WORD AND LAW. AND THAT DAY BECAME A SACRED DAY TO THE LORD.

SCRIPTURE REFERENCE: NEHEMIAH 8:9-12

"THEN NEHEMIAH THE GOVERNOR, EZRA THE PRIEST AND SCRIBE, AND THE LEVITES WHO WERE INSTRUCTING THE PEOPLE SAID TO THEM ALL, "THIS DAY IS SACRED TO THE LORD YOUR GOD. DO NOT MOURN OR WEEP." FOR ALL THE PEOPLE HAD BEEN WEEPING AS THEY LISTENED TO THE WORDS OF THE LAW...." ...."THEN ALL THE PEOPLE WENT AWAY TO EAT AND DRINK, TO SEND PORTIONS OF FOOD AND TO CELEBRATE WITH GREAT JOY, BECAUSE THEY NOW UNDERSTOOD THE WORDS THAT HAD BEEN MADE KNOWN TO THEM."

MOTIVATIONAL MINUTE: LIFT YOUR HANDS IN PRAISE AND YOUR VOICE IN SONG. SATAN CANNOT DEFEAT A WORSHIPPER.

HOW COME THE ISRAELITES MADE A NEW AGREEMENT WITH GOD?

ANSWER:

THE ISRAELITES ASSEMBLED TOGETHER IN ORDER TO CONFESS THEIR SINS TO GOD. AFTER THEY CONFESSED ALL OF THEIR SINS, THEY MADE A BINDING AGREEMENT IN WRITING TO GOD. THE PRIESTS, LEVITES, GATEKEEPERS, SINGERS, TEMPLE SERVANTS AND OTHERS, PROMISED TO FOLLOW THE LAW OF GOD AND TO OBEY HIS COMMANDS, REGULATIONS, AND DECREES. THEY ALSO PROMISED TO TAKE CARE OF GOD'S TEMPLE.

SCRIPTURE REFERENCE: NEHEMIAH 9:38, 10:28-29

"IN VIEW OF ALL THIS, WE ARE MAKING A BINDING AGREEMENT, PUTTING IT IN WRITING, AND OUR LEADERS, OUR LEVITES AND OUR PRIESTS ARE AFFIXING THEIR SEALS TO IT." ....."ALL THESE NOW JOIN THEIR BROTHERS THE NOBLES, AND BIND THEMSELVES WITH A CURSE AND AN OATH TO FOLLOW THE LAW OF GOD GIVEN THROUGH MOSES THE SERVANT OF GOD AND TO OBEY CAREFULLY ALL THE COMMANDS, REGULATIONS AND DECREES OF THE LORD OUR LORD."

MOTIVATIONAL MINUTE: WORDS ARE CONTAINERS FOR POWER. CAREFULLY WATCH OVER YOUR WORDS AND WALK THROUGH LIFE WITH ABUNDANT JOY!

WHY DID NEHEMIAH HAVE TO REFORM THE ISRAELITES AGAIN?

Answer:

Nehemiah had returned to work for King Artaxerxes. Some time later, he asked permission to go back to Jerusalem. When he returned, he discovered that Tobiah, who was forbidden to live in Jerusalem, was living in a room in the house of God. He immediately removed him and put the equipment, grain and incense offerings back into the house. He also discovered that the portions, that were supposed to be given to the Levites, were not given to them, and they had gone back to their own fields. But Nehemiah called them back, and put them back on their posts, at the house of God. The people were also selling goods on the Sabbath day, which was a holy day. And Nehemiah ordered that the gates be shut, until the Sabbath day was over, to keep the day holy.

Scripture Reference: Nehemiah 13:6-11, 19-22

"But while all this was going on, I was not in Jerusalem, for in the thirty-second year of Artaxerxes king of Babylon I had returned to the king. Some time later I asked his permission and came back to Jerusalem...." ...."When evening shadows fell on the gates of Jerusalem before the Sabbath, I ordered the doors to be shut and not opened until the Sabbath was over. I stationed some of my own men at the gates so that no load could be brought in on the Sabbath day...."

MOTIVATIONAL MINUTE: Discouragement destroys hope, so naturally the devil always tries to discourage you.

ESTHER – THE HIDDEN STAR

WHY DID KING XERXES TAKE AWAY QUEEN VASHTI'S CROWN?

ANSWER:

KING XERXES HELD A BANQUET FOR ALL THE NOBLES AND OFFICIALS IN SUSA. QUEEN VASHTI ALSO HAD A BANQUET FOR THE WOMEN IN THE ROYAL PALACE. KING XERXES THOUGHT QUEEN VASHTI WAS BEAUTIFUL, AND WANTED HER TO COME TO HIS BANQUET SO ALL OF THE OFFICIALS COULD SEE HER. SHE REFUSED AND KING XERXES BECAME VERY ANGRY. BECAUSE OF HIS ANGER AND LOSS OF RESPECT, HE ORDERED THAT QUEEN VASHTI NEVER SEE HIM AGAIN, AND FOR HER POSITION TO BE GIVEN TO SOMEONE ELSE. KING XERXES DID THIS SO ALL OF THE WIVES IN THE KINGDOM, WOULD RESPECT THEIR HUSBANDS AND HE WOULD RULE OVER HIS HOUSEHOLD.

SCRIPTURE REFERENCE: ESTHER 1:10-12, 19-20

"ON THE SEVENTH DAY, WHEN KING XERXES WAS IN HIGH SPIRITS FROM WINE, HE COMMANDED THE SEVEN EUNUCHS WHO SERVED HIM- MEHUMAN, BIZTHA, HARBONA, BIGTHA, ABAGTHA, ZETHAR AND CARCAS- TO BRING BEFORE HIM QUEEN VASHTI, WEARING HER ROYAL CROWN, IN ORDER TO DISPLAY HER BEAUTY TO THE PEOPLE AND NOBLES, FOR SHE WAS LOVELY TO LOOK AT. BUT WHEN THE ATTENDANTS DELIVERED THE KING'S COMMAND, QUEEN VASHTI REFUSED TO COME. THEN THE KING BECAME FURIOUS AND BURNED WITH ANGER."

MOTIVATIONAL MINUTE: IF YOU INTEND TO MAKE LOVE A HABIT, YOU MUST DEVELOP THE HABIT OF LOVING PEOPLE WITH YOUR WORDS.

HOW DID ESTHER, A JEW, BECOME QUEEN?

Answer:

After King Xerxes removed Queen Vashti, he started to miss her. So the king's assistants proposed that he look for a new, beautiful, young virgin, to be queen. After the king's approval, they had many girls brought to the palace. Esther was a Jew and was raised by her uncle, Mordecai. Mordecai told Esther not to tell the king that she was Jewish. When it was time for Esther to go see the king, he was attracted to her. So he put the crown on her head, made her the new queen, and gave a great banquet and holiday in her name.

Scripture Reference: Esther 2:1-7, 17

"Later when the anger of King Xerxes had subsided, he remembered Vashti and what she had done and what he had decreed about her. Then the king's personal attendants proposed. "Let a search be made for beautiful young virgins for the king. Let the king appoint commissioners in every province of his realm to bring all these beautiful girls into the harem at the citadel of Susa. Let them be placed under the care of Hegai, the king's eunuch, who is in charge of the women; and let beauty treatments be given to them..." ...."Mordecai had a cousin named Hadassah, whom he had brought up because she had neither father nor mother. This girl, who was also known as Esther, was lovely in form and features, and Mordecai had taken her as his own daughter when her father and mother died...." ...."Now the king was attracted to Esther more than to any of the other women, and she won his favor and approval more than any of the other virgins. So he set a royal crown on her head and made her queen instead of Vashti."

MOTIVATIONAL MINUTE: Life can be difficult, but God will always intervene and his help will always arrive on time.

WHY DID HAMAN WANT TO KILL ALL OF THE JEWISH PEOPLE?

Answer:

King Xerxes gave Haman a seat of honor, which was the highest honor of his officials. The king ordered that everyone kneel down to pay Haman honor, but Esther's uncle, Mordecai, refused to do so. When Haman found out, he became angry. Instead of killing Mordecai, he looked for a way to kill the Jews throughout the whole kingdom. And he selected a month and day to do so.

Scripture Reference: Esther 3:1-7

"After these events, King Xerxes honored Haman son of Hammedatha, the Agagite, elevating him and giving him a seat of honor higher than that of all the other nobles. All the royal officials at the king's gate knelt down and paid honor to Haman, for the king had commanded this concerning him. But Mordecai would not kneel down or pay him honor. Then the royal officials at the king's gate asked Mordecai. "Why do you disobey the king's command?" Day after day they spoke to him but he refused to comply. Therefore they told Haman about it to see whether Mordecai's behavior would be tolerated, for he had told them he was a Jew...." ...."Yet having learned who Mordecai's people were, he scorned the idea of killing only Mordecai. Instead Haman looked for a way to destroy all Mordecai's people, the Jews, throughout the whole kingdom of Xerxes...."

MOTIVATIONAL MINUTE: Whether it is an eating disorder or a temper, you cannot blame it on your genes or your family.

WHY DID KING XERXES KILL HAMAN?

Answer:

AFTER MORDECAI TOLD QUEEN ESTHER THAT HAMAN'S PLAN WAS TO KILL THE JEWS, SHE PRAYED AND DECIDED TO HAVE A BANQUET FOR KING XERXES AND HAMAN. THE KING HAD ALREADY HONORED MORDECAI, BECAUSE HE SAVED THE KING FROM BEING ASSASSINATED. SO WHEN ESTHER HELD THE BANQUET, SHE TOLD THE KING ABOUT HAMAN'S PLAN TO KILL THE JEWS. BECAUSE THE KING BECAME SO ANGRY, AND THOUGHT THAT HAMAN COULD MOLEST ESTHER, HE ORDERED THAT HAMAN BE HUNG ON THE SEVENTY-FIVE FOOT GALLOW THAT HE HAD MADE FOR MORDECAI .

SCRIPTURE REFERENCE: ESTHER 7:3-6, 9-10

"THEN QUEEN ESTHER ANSWERED, "IF I HAVE FOUND FAVOR WITH YOU, O KING, AND IF IT PLEASES YOUR MAJESTY, GRANT ME MY LIFE- THIS IS MY PETITION. AND SPARE MY PEOPLE- THIS IS MY REQUEST. FOR I AND MY PEOPLE HAVE BEEN SOLD FOR DESTRUCTION AND SLAUGHTER AND ANNIHILATION. IF WE HAD MERELY BEEN SOLD AS MALE AND FEMALE SLAVES, I WOULD HAVE KEPT QUIET, BECAUSE NO SUCH DISTRESS WOULD JUSTIFY DISTURBING THE KING. KING XERXES ASKED QUEEN ESTHER, "WHO IS HE?" "WHERE IS THE MAN WHO HAS DARED TO DO SUCH A THING?" ESTHER SAID, "THE ADVERSARY AND ENEMY IS THIS VILE HAMAN." "THEN HAMAN WAS TERRIFIED BEFORE THE KING AND QUEEN." ...."THEN HARBONA, ONE OF THE EUNUCHS ATTENDING THE KING, SAID, "A GALLOWS SEVENTY-FIVE FEET HIGH STANDS BY HAMAN'S HOUSE. HE HAD IT MADE FOR MORDECAI, WHO SPOKE UP TO HELP THE KING." "THE KING SAID, "HANG HIM ON IT!" SO THEY HANGED HAMAN ON THE GALLOWS HE HAD PREPARED FOR MORDECAI. THEN THE KING'S FURY SUBSIDED."

MOTIVATIONAL MINUTE: FEAR IS A SPIRIT THAT MUST BE CONFRONTED HEAD ON- IT WILL NOT JUST GO AWAY.

WHY DID THE JEWS CELEBRATE PURIM?

Answer:

After Haman was killed, Mordecai sent letters throughout the kingdom to annually celebrate the fourteenth and fifteenth days of the month of Adar. This was the time that the Jews lives were spared from their enemies. Because their enemies had plotted and cast the "pur" or the lot, to destroy them. Since King Xerxes ordered the deaths of their enemies, including the ten sons of Haman, they called the celebration Purim, which came from the word "pur," to be remembered and observed for generations to come.

Scripture Reference: Esther 9:23-27

"So the Jews agreed to continue the celebration they had begun, doing what Mordecai had written to them. For Haman son of Hammedatha, the Agagite, the enemy of all the Jews, had plotted against the Jews to destroy them and had cast the *pur* (that is, the lot) for their ruin and destruction. But when the plot came to the king's attention, he issued written orders that the evil scheme Haman had devised against the Jews should come back onto his own head, and that he and his sons should be hanged on the gallows. (Therefore these days were called Purim, from the word *pur*.) ...."The Jews took it upon themselves to establish the custom that they and their descendants and all who join them should without fail observe these two days every year, in the way prescribed and at the time appointed."

Motivational Minute: God is so great, there is no way for us to describe Him properly.

www.ingramcontent.com/pod-product-compliance
Lightning Source LLC
Chambersburg PA
CBHW071308060426
42444CB00034B/1328